ELIZABETH KUSTER

A FIRESIDE BOOK

Published by Simon & Schuster

New York   London   Toronto   Sydney   Tokyo   Singapore

Exorcising Your Ex

How to Get Rid of the Demons
of Relationships Past

FIRESIDE
Rockefeller Center
1230 Avenue of the Americas
New York, NY 10020

FIRESIDE and colophon are registered trademarks
of Simon & Schuster Inc.

Designed by Katy Riegel
Manufactured in the United States of America

1   3   5   7   9   10   8   6   4   2

Library of Congress Cataloging-in-Publication Data
Kuster, Elizabeth.
Exorcising your ex : how to get rid of the demons of relationships
past / Elizabeth Kuster.
p.   cm.
1. Single women—Psychology.   2. Separation (Psychology)   3. Man-
woman relationships.   4. Dating (Social customs)   I. Title.
HQ800.2.K87   1996
646.7'008652—dc20   95-42614
CIP

ISBN 0-684-80302-X

This book is dedicated to you, the reader.
May it give you courage,
hope, and, above all, solace.

Contents

Contents

Disclaimer

When word got around that I was writing a book about ex-boyfriends, several male relatives took me aside. Most of our conversations went something like this:

MALE RELATIVE: I hear you're writing a book about ex-boyfriends.
ME: Yup.
MALE RELATIVE: I sure hope it's not going to be one of those *man-bashing* books.
ME: Of course not. It's not even going to be a hardcover book, so, believe me, it will not be used for any *man bashing*.
MALE RELATIVE (*nervously*): Ha ha.

Bad jokes aside, I would hereby like to announce that this is *not* a man-bashing book. It's an *ex-boyfriend*–bashing book. There is a big difference. Being an intelligent person, I know that just because every guy *I've* dated was (and probably still is) a cretin doesn't mean that all guys are cretins. I mean, think how unfair it would be if all *women* had to take the rap for, say, Sean Young, who allegedly Krazy-Glued James Woods' penis to his thigh after he broke up with her.

The *real* purpose of this book is to help women get over guys who were wrong for them so they can have a good relationship with a guy who's right for them. As one woman put it, "There's a difference between being smart and being bitter. I'm still willing to be blown away by a guy."

I share this woman's hope that there's a guy out there who's just right for me, a guy who preferably does not like to sit on the toilet and read the entire *New York Times* Sunday paper. This guy may live in Addis Ababa, land of the dark and uncomfortable outdoor toilets, but he's out there somewhere.

That said, I would now like to announce the following:

▲ Any similarity between men described in this book and Beavis, Butt-head, or any member of the Three Stooges is entirely coincidental.

▲ Any similarity between men described in this book and actual ex-boyfriends of mine is just too damn bad.

▲ In some cases, names and situations have been altered to protect me from lawsuits or ugly, embarrassing scenes involving said ex-boyfriends.

Introduction

MAYBE IT WAS mutual, or maybe he left you. Maybe you caught him doing something so unbelievably horrifying—chewing his toenails, embezzling money, leering at the babes from *Beverly Hills 90210*—that you couldn't stand the sight of him for one more second. Whatever the reason for the parting, it's done. He's gone, you're alone, and you are just realizing that, sooner or later, you'll have to get naked in front of *someone else*.

Bummer.

Let's face it: Breakups suck. They rank right up there with car wrecks, menstrual cramps, and really bad infomercials.

But hey, look at the bright side: You'll never have to watch *All-Star Wrestling* again!

Just kidding. Actually, the bright side is this: Each bad relationship you go through brings you closer to having the relationship you really want. If, say, you date a man who has bad hygiene and bad grammar and refuses to help you clean, next time you might date a guy who has bad hygiene and bad grammar but who'll walk his dirty dishes to the sink. Besides, in this day and age, when women are dating several guys instead of marrying the proverbial high school sweetheart, getting over a man has become a veritable rite of passage. (If we were men, we'd high-five here.)

By now you're probably wondering what makes me such an expert. Well, let's just say that if this book were called *How to Make Your Relationship Last*, it would have to be plagiarized: The average magazine subscription lasts twice as long as most of my relationships.

Getting over guys—now *that's* where I'm experienced. I've dated them all: the impotent, the asinine, the self-absorbed, the incredibly boring. Many of my ex-boyfriends, in fact, could star in my private version of *Snow White and the Seven Dwarfs*, with the dwarfs being Dopey, Jerky, Crappy, Sleazy, Sneaky, Woeful, and Cheap.

Let's take a friendly tour through a few of my past relationships (and I use that term loosely).

IMPORTANT DATING TIP #1: Don't date until you're at least thirty. In college, I went out with a guy who broke into the biology lab and stole the scales, stepping on various embalmed animals in the process. A few weeks later, my biology teacher separated our class into two groups and put her hands behind her back. "Okay, pick a hand," she said to my group. We did. "It's your lucky day!" she cried. "You get to dissect the rat that Beth's boyfriend *didn't* step on!" The class booed. They wanted me to get the rat that was smashed flatter than a pancake.

IMPORTANT DATING TIP #2: Never date your next-door neighbor. A few years later, I dated my next-door neighbor, a guy who loved to go hunting. I honestly don't remember why we broke up, but for months afterward, he would note my comings and goings through his peephole. If he saw me with another guy, he'd put the bloody foot of a pheasant on my doorknob. (Dead animals are a recurring theme in my early relationships.)

IMPORTANT DATING TIP #3: "I need some space" always means "This planet isn't big enough for the both of us, so if you don't leave me alone I'm going to stow away on the next shuttle flight." After college, I dated a guy I was absolutely crazy about. Six months into our relationship, he told me that he wanted to marry me but first he needed some space. "I don't know how long it will be, but please trust me," he said. "I love you and want to be with you forever. Just don't call me. Wait until I call you."

That was the last I ever heard from *him*.

These are but three examples. I have also dated a guy who kissed me with his mouth open so wide I got bite marks on my cheeks, a guy whose favorite saying was, "White men are the most discriminated-against group in this country," and a guy who put up my Christmas tree so ineptly that it fell down not once but three times—and who, in the process of putting it back up again, stomped merrily on my treasured ornaments as if they were grapes and he was making wine. Not to mention the guy who added up his date expenditures when we got home ("And then you ordered a cappuccino, so that means I spent $78"), the "starving actor" *I* supported who took a trip to Paris a week after we broke up, and the guy I'll call The Screamer, for reasons we need not mention.

The two important lessons I have learned:

1. Boy, does my judgment stink.
2. The sooner you get over Mr. Wrong, the sooner you can move on to the next Big Loser.

That's where this book comes in. Inside, you'll find age-old wisdom that has been passed down through the centuries via secret female tribal rituals involving Ouija boards, Barbie dolls, and marathon sessions of Truth-or-Dare.

Just kidding. Actually, you'll find real-life tricks and techniques from fifty women who've survived bad breakups. Our collective hope: This book will help you get over those nagging negative memories quickly, effectively, painlessly. And failing that, it'll give you a few cheap laughs.

So get into your footie pajamas, make a cup of tea, grab a box of Kleenex—and read on.

Part One

The First Four Months:

Welcome to Hell

8 Signs That You're Suffering from a Traumatic Breakup

▲ You spent last weekend polishing your paper clips and putting your albums, cassettes, and CDs into alphabetical order.

▲ You no longer have the song "Nothing Compares 2 U" because you played it so much that your tape player ate it.

▲ Your apartment is either so clean you could make iced tea from the water in the toilet or so dirty it would make a garbage dump look like the Plaza Hotel.

▲ You see your ex's face when you look at your bus driver, your butcher, your dog.*

▲ You drive by your ex's house so often that you've worn a groove into the asphalt.

▲ Your personal hygiene has deteriorated to the point that animals and small children run away, yelping, as soon as you come within smelling distance.

▲ You've made so many hang-up calls to your ex that you have a callus on your index finger.

▲ While reading this list, you went through an entire box of Kleenex.

*It's like that *Twilight Zone* episode in which Richard Long played all the guy parts. Everywhere you turn: Number 17! Number 17!

1

The Aftermath

An A-to-Z Guide to Post-Breakup Mood Swings

> **Warning:** You will be experiencing fits of rage, helpless laughter, and projectile sobbing, often simultaneously.

 IN THE PERIOD immediately following a breakup, every emotion in the book will rear its ugly head. One minute you will feel lazy, sleepy, depressed; the next you will feel productive, energetic, euphoric. One minute you will feel like killing your ex in a murderous rage; the next you will feel like eating a big hoagie.

Lest you think that any of these emotions are weird or psychotic, let me assure

 "After the breakup, I couldn't eat or speak for days. I cried whenever anyone even mentioned his name."
—Erin, New York City

you that *of course they are!* They're also quite normal—for someone who's just suffered a breakup.

Here are some of the post-breakup emotions and urges you may experience:

A: Anger. Not only will you be angry at yourself, your ex, and the world at large, you'll also be angry at anyone who smiles at you, tells you to cheer up, or says hello. (*Tip:* Avoid Hare Krishnas.)

B: Blame. At first, you'll be tempted to blame yourself for the breakup. Therapists say this is necessary and even healthy, because it makes you feel like you have control over what happens to you. I say forget all that: It's much more fun to blame others. Blaming your ex is, of course, a given. Other good people to blame: ▲ Your parents. ▲ Saddam Hussein. ▲ Howard Stern. And don't forget those old blame standbys ▲ overpopulation, ▲ the greenhouse effect, and ▲ bad karma. If all else fails, ▲ blame PMS.

C: The urge to **clean.** I'm not talking about your average everyday dusting and sweeping here. I'm talking about a cleaning *frenzy.* Not only will you find yourself vacuuming the inside of your file cabinet, you will find yourself vacuuming *inside each file folder.* If you have any empty envelopes in your apartment, you will *vacuum them out, too.* And this is *after* you've cleaned the inside of your mailbox and dusted every book you own, page by page.

Cleaning is therapeutic, true. But I think the real impetus behind the post-breakup cleaning frenzy is the desperate urge to get rid of *every single skin flake your ex ever shed in your apartment.*

D: At some point, you will feel like **drinking your-self silly.** While going on a bender can be self-destructive, it's also an excellent anesthetic. (They don't call it "drowning your sorrows" for nothing.) Remember: Alcohol *kills brain cells.* Killing brain cells results in *memory loss.* Therefore, if you drink enough alcohol, you will eventually *forget that your ex ever existed.*

Tip: Don't make drinking too much of a habit, or you will be spending a good portion of your life waiting for aspirin to work.

E: Embarrassment. After anger, this is probably the most common post-breakup emotion. Women I talked to reported feeling "embarrassed that I fell for my ex's lines," "embarrassed that I gushed about him to friends and family," and "embarrassed that I saw the box of tampons in his bathroom and didn't get the clue." Some were mortified about things they did during the actual breakup. "I literally got down on my knees and begged him not to leave me," said one woman. "It kills me to think that his last view of me was so pathetic." Another woman drove by her ex's house at least four times a day. "He lived at the end of a dead-end street, so every time I drove by, I had to do a three-point turn in his driveway," she said. "He finally came out and told me to stop it."

F: You will feel **free.** Suddenly, your life will be filled with new options. Any behavior that your boyfriend loathed can now become part of your daily repertoire. Hooray! You can eat cookies in bed! You can eat Chef Boyardee ravioli right out of the can! Wear your rattiest underwear! Play your *Saturday Night Fever* album! Let the dishes pile up! Yay! No more pretending that you like his mother! No more little hairs in the bathroom sink! No more empty ice trays!

You will enjoy this newfound freedom for about ten minutes. Then you will burst into tears.

G: Guilt. If you were the one who did the breaking up, you will feel very guilty. Don't let this get you down! Remember, guilt is the basis for all that's good in the world (namely, sex, religion, and *Court TV*).

H: Hunger. After the breakup, some of your pain may be referred to your stomach, which will respond by screaming, "Feed me! Feed me till I explode!" These screams will be followed by intense cravings for various comfort foods (defined as "processed foods, typically bright orange in color, which are highly unhealthy and therefore incredibly expensive").

I myself have experienced this phenomenon. After one breakup, I wandered through the grocery store in a virtual daze for two whole hours. When I got home and started putting the food away, I thought at first that I'd grabbed someone else's bags by mistake. There were *three* boxes of kids' cereal, a jar of Peter Pan peanut butter, two boxes of Kraft macaroni and cheese, a jar of Clausen dill pickles, and a jar of Marshmallow Fluff. Yes, *Marshmallow Fluff!* Apparently my inner child had done the shopping.

Some women say that they actually *lose* their appetite after a breakup. I'd like to smack them, but I don't think I can roll off the couch.

I: You will feel **impulsive.** You will hunger for new experiences, especially those that would shock your ex. "Belly dancing class? Sounds great!" "Skydiving? Sure!" "A full-body tattoo of the Leaning Tower of Pisa? I'm ready!" (*Tip:* Stay away from army recruiters while you are in this frame of mind.)

Note: After a breakup, you may also feel **ill.** According to one therapist, "Many wounded people experience physical symptoms. Some suffer headaches, sleeplessness, hallucinations, rectal bleeding, and gastrointestinal problems."

To which I reply: *Rectal bleeding?!?* Ewww!

J: Jealousy. Typical causes of post-breakup jealousy: ▲ Seeing your ex with the woman he dumped you for. ▲ Seeing your ex enjoying himself with his friends. ▲ Seeing a guy who *looks* like your ex enjoying himself. ▲ Seeing any couple who looks at all happy.

Note: Breaking up with a guy will not prevent you from feeling jealous. As one woman put it, "When I saw my ex with another woman the week after I broke up with him, I was insanely jealous. I couldn't believe that he could get over me that quickly."

K: You will want to give your ex a **knuckle sandwich.** One woman found this urge so overwhelming that she joined a **kung fu class** so she could release this negative energy in a safe environment. Then she proceeded to **kick the shit** out of her instructor.

L: Lots of people **laugh** when they're nervous or upset; it's sort of a survival instinct. After a breakup, the strangest things may set you off. "I'm going to be alone for the rest of my life," you'll be thinking. Suddenly you'll have a vision of your eighty-year-old self buying Depends undergarments, and you'll start laughing so hysterically that nearby strangers will pound you on the back.

Tip: People won't understand that while you may be laughing on the outside, you are actually crying on the inside. Therefore, it might be a good idea to carry a Watchman with you at all times. That way, whenever you're struck by a sudden giggle fit, you can point to the tiny TV screen and pretend that someone on a sitcom just said something funny. Of course, this will probably require **lying.**

M: Memories. Everything you see and hear for those first few weeks—Hungry Man TV dinners, Calvin Klein commercials, the **Muzak** version of "**Muskrat Love**"—will remind you of your ex. For one woman, it was Teva sandals. "My boyfriend wore them all the time, and I *hated* them," she said. "Then, after we broke up, I saw them in a store window. One minute I was fine, and the next minute I was sobbing hysterically." For another woman, it was seeing a guy *spit*. "My ex could spit really high in the air and then catch it in his mouth, like Judd Nelson did in *The Breakfast Club*," she said. "He could plan it so that the spit would land on my head no matter where I dodged. It was so cool."

Tip: Whenever warm memories like these come back to you, *immediately* replace them with a mental picture of your ex at his most disgusting, stupid, and infuriating (preferably all three). Remember how he grunted while watching the bikini-clad women on *Baywatch?* Good. All pleasant thoughts of him should now be flying right out of your head.

N: You will feel like you've reached your **nadir,** or lowest point. (Not to be confused with *Ralph* Nader.) Then you will feel like taking a **nap.**

O: You will feel like composing an **ode** to your ex. The ode will probably start out polite, but eventually it will degenerate into **obscene oaths.** *Do not mail this ode to your ex!*

Note: If writing an ode seems too highbrow, try writing a limerick. Here's one to get you started:

> There once was a man from Venus
> Who fell in love with his penis.
> I wasn't impressed
> (It was four inches at best)
> And so I said, "Been there, seen this."

P: Phobic. Common post-breakup phobias: androphobia (fear of men); anuptaphobia (fear of being single); genophobia (fear of sex); bromidrosiphobia (fear of body odors, real or imagined*). Worst-case scenario: genoandrobromidrosiphobia (fear of having sex with a man who has body odor).

Note: If you ignored my advice and mailed your ode to your ex, you will no doubt be writing a **palinode** (in lay terms, a poem retracting something said in an earlier poem).

Tip: If you're looking for something that rhymes with "sorry," try "Mata Hari."

Q: You will feel like **quitting the relationship thing altogether.** Even keeping a cactus will seem like too much of a commitment.

R: Regret. If your ex was nice, you will regret the times

---

*Possible imagined body odors: crayon, lima bean, rubber cement, new-car smell.

you were mean to him. If he was mean, you will regret the times that you were nice to him. If he was really, really mean, you will regret giving him your phone number in the first place.

S: You will feel **suicidal.** After a breakup, I have been known to say to friends, "Should I meet you there, or should I stay home and slit my wrists?" and, "I would fling myself out the window, but I live on the first floor."

Before you do anything drastic, consider this: Isn't it possible that, instead of wanting to kill yourself, you really just want to kill that little part of you that still likes your ex? If so, why should the rest of you suffer?

I say, be kind to yourself. Treat yourself to a **shopping spree,** preferably with your ex's credit card.

T: Lack of **trust.** After a breakup, you may become suspicious of everyone and everything. This is known as Richard Nixon complex.

Scenario: A new guy asks you out. Your thoughts: ▲ "This guy just wants to get into my pants." ▲ "This guy is just trying to find out where I live, so he can rob me blind." ▲ "My ex must have sent this guy to spy on me."

This lack of trust may be accompanied by the belief that everything is **trivial.**

Scenario: Your boss says, "Remember, we're meeting with our biggest client tomorrow." Your reply: "Who cares? It's not like we're doing *brain surgery* here."

Scenario: Your best friend says, "Brad Pitt is *completely nude* in his next movie!" Your reply: "Big deal. In two billion years, the sun will explode and the world as we know it will cease to exist."

Note: One positive side effect of this fatalistic attitude is that it will depress everyone around you, including your **therapist.**

U: You will feel **undesirable, unbalanced, unapproachable, unappealing,** and just plain **un.** These feelings will make you so apathetic that you will stop shaving your **underarms.** Your roommate will endure your sprouting tufts of armpit hair for about three weeks before screaming **"uncle."**

V: You will fantasize about going on a **vindictive vendetta** against your ex, preferably one that involves performing a **vasectomy** with a **very dull knife.**

Tip: Before following through on this fantasy, read the upcoming chapter on revenge.

W: Withdrawal symptoms. When we're in love, our bodies produce an amphetamine called phenylethylamine. Amphetamines are addictive. Therefore, it follows that you might experience withdrawal symptoms when love ends. Kicking this "relationship habit" will take time. To speed up the process, you could try following the 12-step program recommended by Alcoholics Anonymous. Or you could follow *my* 12-step program, otherwise known as the "12 Steps to the Refrigerator" program (see "H," above).

Note: Even habits that make you feel *awful* can be comforting because they're familiar. So try not to get into the habit of whining about your ex. Otherwise, your friends and family may get into the habit of avoiding you like the plague.

X: You will hate anyone who has only one **X chromosome.** If your bagel man says, "Have a nice day," you'll reply, "Screw you!" If your male doctor asks, "How are you feeling?," you'll snarl, "What's it to ya?" If your dad asks you if you want to go to a movie, you'll shout, "Scram, you testosterone terrorist! I'm sick of your kind!"

Note: Though usually short-lived, this phase is incredibly powerful. Some of its better-known results: ▲ The feminist movement. ▲ Satin-touch tampons. ▲ Susan Powter.

Y: You will feel like **yelling.** Yelling is very cathartic, so you should indulge this urge to the fullest. Good places to yell: ▲ your car, ▲ your pillow, ▲ **Yankee Stadium.** Bad places to yell: ▲ the library, ▲ the police station, ▲ church.

Note: The urge to yell at weddings is quite understandable, but it's still not appropriate.

Z: You will feel like a **zombie.**

'zäm-be, *noun.* **1.** A voodoo snake deity. **2.** A person held to resemble the so-called walking dead; esp: AUTOMA-TON. **3.** A person markedly strange in appearance or behavior. **4.** A mixed drink made of several kinds of rum, liqueur, and fruit juice.

The Wild and Wacky Things That Remind Women of Their Exes

▲ "*Star Wars,* Don Mattingly, and the entire state of Iowa."

▲ "Lubricant."

▲ "The Stevie Nicks song 'Rhiannon'. He said I reminded him of Rhiannon. I later found out that Rhiannon was the name of a witch who ate her two children."

▲ "Ugly ties, chewing tobacco, and Frank Sinatra."

▲ "Vinegar. He loved it so much he drank it right out of the bottle."

▲ "Oscar de la Renta perfume. The night we broke up, I threw my brand-new bottle at him. It broke and soaked the carpet in my bedroom. I had to smell it for months."

▲ "*Platoon.* It was the only movie he took me to in the three years we dated."

▲ "Ryder trucks. They remind me of the time we moved cross-country together. Whenever I see one now, I want to run it off the road."

▲ "The 'Happy Birthday' song." (Considering that this is the world's most frequently sung song, this is a *real* drag.)

▲ "Roast beef and cheese sandwiches. That's what I had for lunch the day my divorce was final."

▲ "Avocado green. It was the color of his clunky '67 Dodge."

▲ "Spaghetti and meatballs."

▲ "Leather chairs. He had a leather chair that he was very anal about; he came unglued if I even set my purse on it. Now when I see a leather chair, I plop right down."

▲ "The smell of Dallas."

▲ "*Hustler* magazine and the Three Stooges."

▲ "Putty things—you know, those tools."

2

"When Will the Pain Stop?"

MANY OF THE WOMEN I interviewed asked me this question. I told them what I'll tell you: Most experts say it takes half the amount of time that you dated to get over a guy. Wait—maybe the theory is that it takes *twice* the amount of time you dated to get over a guy. I can never quite remember, but I know it's kind of like figuring dog years. Anyway, according to this theory, if you dated your ex for ten years, it will take you either five or twenty years to get over him.

After serious consideration, I think it's pretty clear that this theory, whatever it is, doesn't hold water. (You may now breathe a huge sigh of relief.) Why? Because every relationship is different. As you'll see in future chapters, women sometimes stay with guys long after they feel like breaking up with them, for all sorts of reasons (habit, laziness, the fear that they'll starve if they don't have a guy around to open jars for them, etc.). Should this period be figured into

31

the post-breakup equation? I think not. When it comes to getting over a guy, it's the quality of the relationship that matters—*not* its duration. Therefore, it only follows that if you hated your boyfriend from the very beginning, you should get over him in a snap, even if you, say, married him.

I realize that all of this sounds highly subjective and maybe even dubious, so I have developed my own mathematical equation to help you figure out how long it will take you to get over your ex. As you read it, keep in mind that (1) math was never really my thing, and (2) I made this equation up.

▲▲▲▲▲▲▲▲▲▲▲▲▲▲▲▲▲▲▲▲▲▲▲▲▲

Elizabeth Kuster's Fabulous "How Long Will It Take Me to Get Over Him?" Equation for Women

$$\text{How long} = \frac{\left(\dfrac{s/o}{c}\right)(g+f+v)}{tv/4} \times \frac{b+d}{pig}$$

where

s = number of times you had great sex*

o = number of times you *pretended* to have great sex†

c = number of times he made fun of your cooking

---

*Sex that made you lose your sense of reality to the point that you actually believed, for a moment, that he really *was* Tom Cruise.

†By suddenly jerking awake and yelling, "Oh, *yeah!*"

g = number of nice gifts he bought you

f = number of times he gave you flowers

v = number of times he took you on a tropical vacation*

tv = number of hours he spent watching sports on TV

b = number of gross bugs he killed

d = number of dishes he washed the whole time you dated

pig = number of times he said things like, "White men are the most discriminated-against group in this country."

If, for example, s, b, f, v, and g = 1, o = 20, d = 2, tv = 4000, and c and pig = 10, then it will take you . . .

$$\frac{\left(\dfrac{1/20}{10}\right)(1+1+1)}{4000/4} \times \frac{1+2}{10}$$

$$= \frac{(.005)(3)}{1000} \times \frac{3}{10}$$

$$= .015/1000 \times .3$$

$$= .0000045$$

. . . less than one second to get over your ex.

If, however, o, c, and pig = 1, g and f = 50, s and tv = 100, b and d = 1000, and v = 4, then it will take you . . .

*A trip to Orange Julius does *not* constitute a tropical vacation.

$$\frac{\left(\frac{100/1}{1}\right)(50+50+4)}{100/4} \times \frac{1000+1000}{1}$$

$$= \frac{(100)(104)}{25} \times \frac{2000}{1}$$

$$= 10,400/25 \times 2000$$

$$= 832,000$$

. . . a helluva long time to get over your ex.

There are, of course, countless other factors that can affect your post-breakup recovery time (hereafter known as PBRT). One thing that can shorten your PBRT is what one woman called the Emotional Drāno Effect: having something happen that makes your ex completely repulsive to you.

Here are a few examples:

▲ "Winning the lottery."
▲ "Finding out my ex is dating someone much uglier."
▲ "Hearing that he's gained 40 pounds, has been excommunicated, and has a worthless life devoid of pleasure."
▲ "Finding out my ex has become a chiropractor. He did *not* want to follow in his father's footsteps and once confided to me that if I ever heard he was a chiropractor, I'd know he'd sold out."

One thing that can *lengthen* your PBRT is the fact that our boyfriends and husbands sometimes fulfill more than one of our needs, without our even realizing it. (As one therapist put it, "The loss of a lover means the simultaneous loss of a source for sex, laughter, social support, and intimate talk.") In lay terms, this means that after the breakup, you may be shocked to find that instead of just needing a new Sex Supplier, you also need a new Turkey Carver and Vermin Exterminator, plus a new Emotional Crutch, Verbal Whipping Post, and Butt of Your Jokes. Finding someone new to fill all of these roles can be a real drag and may even take more than ten minutes.

When figuring your PBRT, you must also take into account all of the myriad little things your ex said and did while you dated him and whether or not he was really good-looking. To give you an idea of what I'm talking about, I asked the women I interviewed to tell me what made it harder or easier for *them* to get over a guy. Here are some of their answers.

▲▲▲▲▲▲▲▲▲▲▲▲▲▲▲▲▲▲▲▲▲▲▲▲

It's Harder to Get Over a Guy When . . .

▲ He's like Mel Gibson, only better-looking.

▲ He's scheduled for major surgery (e.g., a kidney transplant) and you promised you'd take care of him (i.e., by giving him one of your kidneys).

▲ You lost your virginity to him. (Especially if you, like one woman, lost your virginity on a gravel road. "No wonder I can't get over him," she says. "I'm still picking rocks out of my back!")

▲ You have his name and/or likeness tattooed on your

> "My ex liked to give me forehead hickeys. I thought no one noticed until a coworker said to me one day, 'Hey, have you got a hickey on your *forehead?!*'"
> —Julie, Iowa City

breasts. (Let us now observe a moment of silence for Roseanne.)

▲ He gave you a chronic STD such as herpes, genital warts, or RGBR (a really gross butt rash).

▲ You bore his child. (I mean bore in the sense that you gave birth, not in the sense that you drone on and on to the kid until his or her little eyes roll back into his or her little head.)

▲ You're related. (One woman I interviewed fell in love with her second cousin. "After we broke up, family reunions were *hell!*" she says.)

▲ He won't move out. (As you'll see in the section on closure, this is not as uncommon as you'd think.)

▲ He fulfilled all of your greatest sexual fantasies, including the one that required him to dress up like Brad Pitt in *Interview with the Vampire* and bite you on the neck.

▲ He did actual exercises designed to improve tongue stamina.

▲ He keeps hiding in your bushes and singing "Unchained Melody."

▲ He has a Polaroid of your erotic nude performance "Me and My Zucchini: A Love Story."

▲▲▲▲▲▲▲▲▲▲▲▲▲▲▲▲▲▲▲▲▲▲▲▲

It's Easier to Get Over a Guy When . . .

▲ The last time you saw him, his neck was covered with hickeys—and they weren't from you.

▲ On your first date, he said, "I'd love to meet some of your girlfriends."

▲ Instead of saying, "My, you look beautiful," he'd say, "My, you look pulchritudinous."

▲ He referred to your private parts as his "tool shed."

▲ Your name is Florence and his last name is Lawrence. (Don't laugh. I know a woman whose married name is Sandy Sandy.)

▲ His idea of foreplay was having you jump naked on his mini-trampoline.

▲ Just when you thought he was going to tell you he loved you, he turned to you and said, "Will you give me a blow job?"

▲ When you called him from vacation and asked if he missed you, he said, "Yes, I miss stroking your ego."

▲ He referred to his mother as "that twit who gave birth to me."

▲ Instead of being hung like a horse, he was hung like a hamster.*

▲ His environmental motto was, "I'd rather kill people than animals."

*Not that size matters.

▲ You found a 38DD bra in his closet, and he said it was the cleaning lady's.
▲ He was a self-proclaimed "vaginophobic."

If after reading all of this you figure that pigs will be ice-skating in hell before you get over your ex, take heart! The strategies described in the next chapter might speed up the process.*

*Then again, they might not.

3

Surviving the First Few Weeks

Small Distractions, Quick Fixes, What *Not* to Do

RIGHT NOW, you're probably thinking about your ex an average of once every second. The good news: By the end of this chapter, you'll be thinking about him once every *other* second. (Hey, it's a start.)

The weeks immediately following a breakup are always the toughest. At this early stage (also known as the Oh-shit-I'm-out-of-Kleenex phase), you *will* run to the window every time a car goes by. You *will* sit by the phone waiting for it to ring, and if one of your friends calls, you *will* respond to her cheerful greeting with, "Oh, it's just *you*."

> "A few weeks after a breakup, I inevitably think I'm pregnant. It's a psychological thing. I think it's based on the fear that I won't be able to get out of a relationship scot-free."
> — Sherry, Santa Fe

In short, you will be absolutely consumed with thoughts of your ex. If you take a Rorschach test, every inkblot will look like him. If you cloud-watch, every *cloud* will look like him. Even the *pepperoni on your pizza* will look like him.

That is why—and this is *very* important—you should avoid being a contestant on *Jeopardy* during this time period. Otherwise, here's what will happen: ▲ You'll frame every answer with the question "Who is my ex?" ▲ Alex Trebek will get really pissed. ▲ You'll be thrown off the show. ▲ You will realize, with horror, that you've just made a fool of yourself on national television *and you weren't even on America's Funniest Home Videos*.

Here are three more important pieces of advice:

1. Don't tell friends and family members how much you're thinking about your ex.

    They will only say things like, "Just put him out of your mind," or, "Whenever you catch yourself thinking about him, visualize a stop sign. Works like a charm." After which you'll have no choice but to choke the daylights out of them.

2. Don't even *try* to stop thinking about your ex.

    Right now, that will be about as do-able as marrying Elvis. (Or for those of you who believe that Elvis is alive and well and working at your neighborhood 7-Eleven, marrying Liberace.) Instead, just try to keep yourself distracted so you don't do something *really* humiliating, such as:

    a. Following your ex around to the point that his friends start calling you The Shadow, or

b. Calling your mother and telling her that she's right—you *are* an incredibly bad judge of character, and if you don't wise up, you will indeed be single for the rest of your life.

3. Remember that Rome wasn't built in a day.

It took *thousands of years* to build Rome. In fact, Rome is *still under construction at this very moment*. This teaches us two very important lessons:

a. Getting over your ex, much like the building of Rome, is a continuous process, and you just have to take it one day at a time, and

b. Boy, those Romans must be pretty slow.

Okay, now that you've accepted the fact that you're going to be plagued with thoughts of your ex for the foreseeable future, it's time to take action. Yes, there are lots of things that you can do to make these first miserable weeks as enjoyable as possible.

So without further ado, I am pleased to present

▲▲▲▲▲▲▲▲▲▲▲▲▲▲▲▲▲▲▲▲▲▲▲▲

Elizabeth Kuster's
Ten Post-Breakup Commandments

THE FIRST COMMANDMENT: Thou shalt *not* get a radical haircut.

Reason #1: Radical haircuts inevitably look ridiculous. *Reason #2:* Looking ridiculous tends to be bad for self-esteem. *Reason #3:* Murphy's Law says that as soon as you come out of the salon, you'll run smack into your ex and he'll say, "Boy, you sure look ridiculous."

True story: I once saw a woman whose hair formed an actual arch over her head, made of two pigtails joined together on top with some kind of glaze. My first thoughts:

▲ This woman has just suffered an extremely traumatic breakup.

▲ This woman has a samurai hairdresser.

▲ Hey! I could play Nerf basketball through the hole in her hair!

Are any of these the image you want to project? I think not. *Note:* There is one—and only one—exception to the haircut rule, and it is this: If you didn't cut your hair because your ex preferred it long, or because he considered your

> "I needed our relationship to end decently before I could move on; my ex had to have it end viciously. We went back and forth for *years.* First we'd end it nicely—and then he'd feel devastated and want me back. Then we'd end it badly, and that would keep *me* hooked in. Finally, to save my soul, I went cold turkey: After one especially bad ending, I just accepted that it wasn't going to end the way I wanted it to, and I stopped answering his calls."
> —Beth, New York

hairstyle to be a personal tribute to his own ego, then you hereby have my permission to run to the bathroom and *shave yourself bald*.

THE SECOND COMMANDMENT: Thou shalt *not* answer the phone. This is very important, because if your ex calls, you may be tempted to say, "No, I'm not busy. I was just playing Scrabble by myself. Want to come over and have sex?" or, "No, I'm not busy. I was just polishing off a pint of Häagen-Dazs, a box of Ho Hos, and a six-pack of beer. Want to come over and have sex?"

Comments like these will show your ex just how desperate and miserable you really are. So instead of answering the phone, put an incredibly upbeat—bordering on sprightly—message on your answering machine. It should sound like you're on the verge of laughing.

Remember my post-breakup motto: "It's okay to feel miserable, as long as your ex doesn't know about it."

THE THIRD COMMAND-MENT: Thou shalt *not* call your ex.
This will be a very tough urge to resist, because you will alternately want to

"I know you're not supposed to make hang-up calls, but . . . I got the voice dialing system, and I've found that it's very therapeutic to pick up the receiver, say 'Scumbucket,' and have his phone ring."
—Elaine, Charleston

▲ Hear his voice,

> "After the breakup, I called my ex because I wanted to get a few things off my chest. I started out nice, but when he didn't listen to me, I got mad and started yelling and he hung up. So I stomped over to his house and started yelling for him to let me in. I was making so much noise that he finally did. I yelled some more—and then he grabbed me by the back of my pants and set me back outside like a sack of potatoes."
> —Tammy, Kansas City

▲ Analyze his answering machine message for hidden meanings,

▲ Leave a nasty message, after which you'll have to call back and apologize, and

▲ Beg him to come over and have sex with you. (See above.)

Stand firm! If these urges start to become overwhelming, try my no-fail anti-calling technique. Here's how it works.

Step 1: Find the worst picture of your ex that you have. Enlarge it. Using a red crayon, draw a circle around your ex's head, and then draw a big red slash through the circle.

Step 2: Make a list of all the awful things your ex ever did or said. When you've exhausted your memory, call all your friends, read them the list, and ask them if they can think of anything you've left out. Add their comments.

Step 3: Xerox the list and the picture so that they're on opposite sides of the same piece of paper. Make lots of copies.

Put one by the phone, one in your purse, and one at your office, and give the rest to friends and family members.

Step 4: When you feel like calling your ex, read the list and look at the picture. If you *still* feel like calling him, call one of your friends and have *her* read the list to you. When she's finished, she will undoubtedly say, "He did all this, and you *still* want to call him?" To which you will be forced to reply, "No. I'm sorry. I don't know *what* I was thinking."

This tactic is a wonderful model of negative reinforcement, and I'm very, very proud to be a part of it. Especially because it really *works*.

Skeptical? I thought you'd be. That's why I asked several women who've used this technique to reveal items from their no-fail anti-calling lists. Here are some of the things they'd written down:

▲ "Whenever I'd ask, 'How do I look?,' he'd say something like, 'Well, you could lose ten pounds/get that mole on your forehead removed/get your teeth whitened.'"

▲ "He stood me up on Valentine's Day and didn't even get me a measly *card*."

▲ "He told me not to wear light blue because it makes me look 'washed-out,' pink because it's 'too frilly and you're not the frilly type,' and black because 'it makes you look so unattractive.'"

▲ "I made him lasagna for dinner one night, and he didn't show up until I'd gone to bed. When he came in, I said, 'Where were you?' and he said, 'Sorry, I forgot.' And I said, 'But I made this great lasagna.' And he said, 'Yeah, I just had a piece. Not enough meat sauce.'"

▲ "He used to call me into the bathroom to show me how to correctly wrap the cord around the hair dryer and put the toilet paper on the holder."

Believe me, after reading a list of transgressions like these, calling your ex will be the *last* thing you'll want to do. You won't feel like being *nice* to him. You won't feel like *having sex* with him. You won't feel like *hearing his voice*. You *will*, however, feel like hearing him shriek when he sees you with a new guy.

THE FOURTH COMMANDMENT: Thou shalt *not* go anywhere your ex might be. Seeing him in public will only make you feel worse, especially if he's with someone else and/or looks as if he's having a good time. (And most especially if you yourself look like a slump-shouldered, sniveling *mess*.)

Yes, this means that, for the next month or so, your movements are going to be limited to Tupperware parties and the Moose Lodge on bingo night. Stop whining and look at the bright side: You now have the perfect excuse to avoid hockey games, frat parties, and monster truck rallies.

Note: I would like to make it very clear that "anywhere your ex might be" does include your ex's *house*. I say this because one woman told me that she kept her ex's keys and went over to his house one night when she was drunk. Upon opening the door, she found her ex in bed with another woman *underneath the Laura Ashley quilt she'd spent a fortune on*. Her ex calmly got out of bed, took some money out of his wallet, and said, without blinking an eye, "Here's money for a cab."

Please, do yourself a favor and *learn from this woman's mistake*.

THE FIFTH COMMANDMENT: Thou shalt use your friends and family. Here are a few suggestions:

▲ Inform them that, should your ex inquire about you, they are to respond, "She's doing *so* great! She's dating some twenty-year-old guy who's in a band. Personally, I think he's too young for her, but she says he's more mature than anyone she's ever dated. Oh—sorry." (For best results, they should memorize this response so that it sounds as natural as possible. You might want to quiz them weekly, just to make sure.)

▲ Remind them that now that *you* hate your ex, *they* have to hate him, too—and that, if they *really* love you, they'll keep hating your ex long after you yourself have forgiven him. Feel free to offer extra points to those friends and relatives who spit on your ex, make disparaging remarks, threaten his life, etc.

▲ Tell them that their new number-one priority is to *get you out of the house*. You must not, at all costs, be allowed to *mope*. If you *do* mope, they are to stop what they're doing—whether it be brain surgery, drag racing, or disposing of nuclear waste—and immediately *take you to the Dairy Queen*.

Using your loved ones in this manner will give them a wonderful opportunity to prove that they really care about you, and that they're not the selfish, uncaring slackers you've always thought they were.

THE SIXTH COMMANDMENT: Thou shalt *not* look up old boyfriends. One woman told me, "When I'm upset about one guy, I usually end up mourning *all* of the guys I've dated. I think, 'Hmm. That one wasn't so bad; maybe I should give him a call.'"

There are many, many reasons why you shouldn't do this.

1. You may learn that your old boyfriend is in prison.
2. You may learn that your old boyfriend is dead.
3. You may learn that your old boyfriend has had a sex-change operation and now goes by the name Daisy Delicious.
4. You may actually go on a date with your old boyfriend, upon which you may learn that he is
   a. bald as a baby's butt, or
   b. an even bigger asshole than he was before.
5. Worst of all, you may learn that your old boyfriend is happily married and has two beautiful children.

THE SEVENTH COMMANDMENT: Thou shalt escape on a fabulous vacation. Take an extended trip to Europe or, if that's too romantic, to a socialist work camp. You'll have a great time, you'll forget all about your ex, and the experience will make you a more interesting and cultured person. Here's how it works:

You've just returned from a fabulous trip to Europe. As you walk into your apartment, the phone rings. You pick up. It's Bob, your ex-boyfriend from hell.

EBFH: Everything was my fault. I love you, I miss you, I can't live without you. Please, please come back to me.
YOU: Who *is* this?

Or, better yet:

You've just returned from a fabulous trip to Europe. As you walk into your apartment, the phone rings. Your gorgeous, sexy, sensitive, and rich new fiancé, Henri—the one you met in Paris and who has moved to the States out of undying love for you—picks up.

GSSRNFH: Allô?
EBFH: Uh . . . is Beth there?
GSSRNFH: Who ees calling?
EBFH: It's Bob.
GSSRNFH (*puts his hand over the receiver*): Eet's for you, darling. Eet's someone called Bob.
YOU: Bob *who?*

Many women I talked to absolutely *swear* by this technique. Here are some of their escape stories:

▲ "After the relationship ended, I flew to St. Thomas, and I sent my ex a very stinging postcard that ended, 'Now I'm going to go sit on the beach. You can sit on this.'"
▲ "I went to Jamaica for a week, alone. I stayed in a pink hotel, bought a tie-dye dress, and tooled around Negril

on a moped. The trip gave me confidence, nourished my soul, and saved my *life*."

▲ "Two hours after the breakup, I packed a bag, went to the airport, and asked for the next flight to a hot place. I ended up in Tomolta, Africa. After two weeks in Tomolta I realized I still wasn't over the guy, so I took out a map of the world and calculated the farthest point from him. Thus began what I like to call 'Mad Mame's World Tour.' I spent a year on the other side of the world, traveling through Tahiti, Australia, Indonesia, Thailand, and Japan. After about 10,000 miles, I started feeling much better."

▲ "I ran to London and went hog-wild with boys. The great thing about escaping to another city is that it gives you a completely new perspective. There's absolutely nothing there to remind you of your ex; your brain is just focusing on the *newness* of it all."

THE EIGHTH COMMANDMENT: Thou shalt rearrange your bedroom. One woman told me, "The day the relationship ends, I move my bed, flip the mattress, and buy new sheets. I don't want to be able to picture my ex in bed with me."

This woman was surprised to learn that, unbeknownst to her, she was practicing the ancient Chinese art of object placement, otherwise known as *feng shui*. According to *feng shui* specialist Nancy SantoPietro, there are several ways to rearrange your bedroom to "clean your aura."

"You'll be in a better position to face lingering relationship issues if you move your bed so it faces the largest part of the room," said SantoPietro. "You should be able to clearly see the doorway without obstructing it. This will align your environment so your personal energy, or *ch'i*, can flow."

My feeling about these and other *feng shui* techniques is, what the hell, you might as well try them. If they don't work, you could always try *my* object-placement technique, which involves inviting your ex over on the pretext of moving furniture and then, when he's not looking, dropping your bureau on his foot.

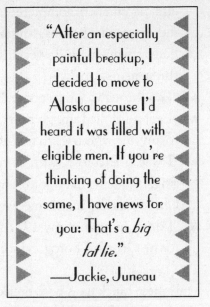

"After an especially painful breakup, I decided to move to Alaska because I'd heard it was filled with eligible men. If you're thinking of doing the same, I have news for you: That's a *big fat lie*."
—Jackie, Juneau

THE NINTH COMMANDMENT: Thou shalt do whatever it takes to cheer yourself up. Think of several little things that would make you feel better. To get you started, here's a list of the small comforts that have helped other women:

▲ "I eat lots and lots of chocolate. They say it has certain chemicals in it that help you feel better, and I believe it."*

▲ "I spend an entire afternoon watching TV talk shows and yelling at the screen. Seeing how *sick* other people are helps me see that my problems are *nothing*."

▲ "I change my perfume. I learned this trick from one of *my* exes: I ran into him a few weeks after we broke up

*For the ultimate chocolate experience, indulge in my patented Yoo-Hoo Diet Plan for Heartbreak (page 54).

and he smelled completely unfamiliar. It really threw me; it was like he was a different person, with a different body chemistry and everything. It will work for you for the same reason."

▲ "I go through a Lycra phase."

▲ "I get all dolled up, go to a fun bar, and act really nasty to any guy who tries to talk to me."

▲ "I watch *Divorce Court*. It makes me very happy to be single, much like going to F.A.O. Schwarz around Christmastime makes me very happy to be childless."

▲ "I drive around in my 1977 sea-green Impala and listen to the George Thorogood song 'Bad to the Bone.'"

I call these quick fixes post-breakup Band-Aids—they won't cure you, but they *will* help you heal faster.

THE TENTH COMMANDMENT: Thou shalt remember that this, too, shall pass. One way to bring this point home is to think back to another time in your life when you felt utterly wretched—the idea being that if you lived through that, you'll live through this, too.

I'll give you an example from my own life. My personal hell? Eighth grade. I had huge brown plastic glasses, a short, curly perm, silver braces, and a flat chest, and I was the only one of my friends who hadn't started her period yet. The boys called me "sunken treasure." I had frequent giggling fits in class. I was just one big quivering mass of hormones with an intense yearning to be popular.

It was during this developmental phase that my parents decided to get a family picture taken at Olan Mills for the one and only time in our family's history. I'll never forget how I felt when the picture came back. There was Dad, looking handsome, happy, not yet gray. There was Mom, looking like the quintessential sexy wife. There was my sister at the peak of her seventeen-year-old beauty: glowing skin, heaving breasts, a smile that would put Disney to shame. And there

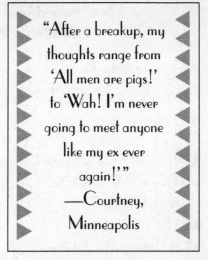

"After a breakup, my thoughts range from 'All men are pigs!' to 'Wah! I'm never going to meet anyone like my ex ever again!'"
—Courtney, Minneapolis

was me, looking like a grinning, prepubescent dork.

My mother hung this picture in the middle of the hallway so people could see it as they came out of the bathroom. I had to beg her to take it down, and she finally did—last summer. Small wonder, then, that after years of looking at this picture, my sister began introducing me to people by saying, "This is my sister. She went through the longest ugly stage of anyone I've ever met."

And so I went from being a fourteen-year-old with a curly perm, a flat chest, and no menstrual cycle to being a twenty-nine-year-old with flat hair, a chest big enough to elicit comments from gross men on the street, and monthly cramps that feel like a white-hot bayonet is being thrust into my gut.

Great. Now *I'm* depressed.

The Yoo-Hoo Diet Plan
for Heartbreak

GUARANTEED TO INDUCE
A CHOCOLATE COMA

INGREDIENTS

▲ 1 six-pack Yoo-Hoo chocolate drink
▲ 1 pint Ben & Jerry's New York Super Fudge Chunk ice cream plus hot fudge sauce
▲ 1 box Hostess Ho Hos
▲ 3 Hershey's chocolate bars
▲ 1 Whitman's Sampler
▲ 1 box Cocoa Pebbles plus a half-gallon of milk
▲ 1 remote control

DIRECTIONS

Sit on your couch. Surround yourself with all ingredients. Turn on your favorite sitcom. Eat until all food is gone or you pass out from the sugar, whichever comes first.

NUTRITION INFORMATION

▲ Vitamins: No
▲ Fat: Yes
▲ Calories: Too damn many

Note: If you follow the Yoo-Hoo Diet Plan for more than three days, skip the upcoming chapter on rebound dating. The only rebound date you'll be getting is when some NBA star mistakes you for a basketball.

4

Revenge

"I'll Stab Your Back, You Stab Mine"

IF YOU'RE THE KIND of woman to whom regret is about as familiar as jock itch *and* you think you could pull off life imprisonment with style and panache, then revenge is the tactic for you. If not, then repeat after me: Revenge is wrong.

Why? Well, I *could* quote the immortal words of Buddy Hackett, who said, "Don't carry a grudge. While you're carrying the grudge, the other guy's out dancing." But you'd probably just think, "What the hell does Buddy Hackett know about revenge?" I could also talk about how damaging it is psychologically and how plotting revenge interferes with your ability to live a happy life, but your response would probably be, "Yeah, yeah. Just tell me where I can get some saltpeter."

So instead I'll say this: It's a hell of a lot easier to get over a man when you're not running from the cops. I know, I know, putting a potato in his exhaust pipe sounds pretty tempting. But will you really feel better when you're in jail and some huge prison matron has singled you out to be her next main squeeze?

If you doubt the validity of these scenarios, remember: Revenge invites retaliation, and men are a *very* retaliatory species (it's all that testosterone). Consider this true story from a thirty-six-year-old graduate student: "After my boyfriend dumped me, I ripped the windshield wipers off his new sports car. He pressed felony charges and had the entire hood repainted. After a nightmarish trial with a male judge who said I needed to be a 'good girl,' I was given probation and restitution charges of over $800." (Which only proves my theory that America's motto is no longer "In God We Trust." It's "I'll sue!")

Okay. Now that I've convinced you that revenge is horrible, evil, and something you should never, ever do, here are some . . .

▲▲▲▲▲▲▲▲▲▲▲▲▲▲▲▲▲▲▲▲▲▲▲▲▲

Nasty Revenge Stories That Are Really Fun to Read Because They Involve People You Don't Know

TRUE REVENGE STORY #1. "I had dated my boyfriend on and off for fifteen years. After he broke up with me, my revenge feelings festered for about a year, to the point that I became completely obsessed with the need to avenge myself. I began keeping a list of all of the C.O.D. products being advertised on TV, and then I started sending in for these products—using my ex's address. In a one-week period I ordered seventeen bamboo steamers, twenty-five complete sets of Ginsu knives, and twenty mattresses from Dial-A-Mattress, among other things. Then I filled out a change-of-address slip at the post office and had all of his mail sent to a fictitious address: 123 Gray Street in Muncie, Indiana. When I ran into my ex on the street a few years later, I noticed that he'd developed a twitch in his eye."

TRUE REVENGE STORY #2. "My therapist works at the same hospital as my ex. After the breakup, I was so devastated that my therapist finally said, 'Look, if you want me to have your ex fired, I can.' It was so *Melrose Place*. In the end, I decided to spare my ex: Knowing that I held his livelihood in the palm of my hand was revenge enough."

TRUE REVENGE STORY #3. "Financial revenge is best, because it gets them where it really burns. My tactic was simple: I took his cable box. Later I learned that he lost his $50 deposit *and* had to pay several hundred dollar's worth of fines."

TRUE REVENGE STORY #4. "When my husband and I split up, I was the one who moved out. He arranged to be out of the house when I came to get my things. I made the most of this opportunity: I put bleach in his Woolite, dumped milk on all of his clothing, and hid pieces of raw meat all over the house."

TRUE REVENGE STORY #5. "My ex was a gardener; he had a dozen huge flowerpots filled with dirt on his patio.

After the breakup, I climbed over his fence, dumped out all of the pots, and then turned on the hose. It made a fabulous mess."

TRUE REVENGE STORY #6. "My ex had gotten me a poinsettia for Christmas. After the breakup, I snuck over to his house and put it behind his back right tire. Then I hid. Eventually he came out, got in the car, and backed over the plant, which made a huge crunching sound. It scared the crap out of him."

TRUE REVENGE STORY #7. "I got a sharp skewer, went to my ex's house, and punctured all four of his tires. Then I came back home and hid the weapon in the dishwasher. I felt pretty good about it—until the next day, when I got run over by a motorcycle. I'm sure it was karma."

TRUE REVENGE STORY #8. "A few years ago I dated this guy I was madly in love with. Well, he turned out to be a big jerk, and when the relationship fell apart, I wanted to make him really, really mad, so I changed all of the women's telephone numbers in his address book—you know, 3s into 8s, 4s into 9s, that kind of thing—and years later I still feel embarrassed and mortified by this and am *really, really sorry, OK???*"

That's the worst thing about revenge: You usually regret it later, even if what you did was technically legal. This said, here are some fun and relatively harmless revenge tactics you could try. They may not be quite as cathartic as the real thing, but trust me: They're much, much safer.

REVENGE TACTIC #1: Sing revenge songs. "I make up new words for old favorites," says one woman. "Instead of, say, 'I Shot the Sheriff,' I sing, 'I shot my boyfriend. But I did not shoot his dog Rufus. Oh yeah, oh yeah.'"

Another woman makes up songs from scratch. "I wrote a great one called 'Instant Pudding, Instant Love Affair, Instant Breakup,'" she says.

Ookay.

REVENGE TACTIC #2: Do some creative writing. "I have a whole computer disc full of sick, twisted horror stories involving mutilation, all of them starring various ex-boyfriends," says one woman. "When I die, friends and family may view these files with horror, muttering in shocked tones about 'psychosis' and 'dementia,' but who cares?"

Tip: If you try this tactic, give the file your ex's name. That way, if you ever decide to erase it, the computer will ask, "Erase Mike?" and you'll get to type, emphatically, "Yes!"

REVENGE TACTIC #3: Make friends with another one of his exes. "I became best friends with my ex's ex-wife," says one woman. "Whenever we're out together and we see him, we sit down next to him and start talking about how he was in bed. It really freaks him out."

REVENGE TACTIC #4: Use your pet. "My boyfriend really loved my dog," says one woman. "When he broke up with me, I told him, 'Geez, now you'll never see the dog again.' My ex became absolutely hysterical."

REVENGE TACTIC #5: Prey on his love of sports. Rent a big-screen TV. Invite your ex over on a day when there are at least ten major games. Arrange for a friend to call just as the first game is about to start. Hang up, and tell your ex you have to run out for a few hours, but that he can stay and watch the games. Then, just before you leave, *hide the remote*. By the time you come back, your ex will be a raging lunatic.

REVENGE TACTIC #6: Put a curse on him. "Men are very gullible," notes one woman. "When my ex broke up with me, I told him that if he ever gave oral sex to someone else, he'd get vertigo. Apparently he bought it, because two years later I met his new girlfriend and she complained that he wouldn't give her oral sex because he said it made him feel dizzy!"

REVENGE TACTIC #7: Tell your story to the tabloids. Celebrities are really good at revenge. I know, because I read it in *People*. That's where I learned that

▲ After Woody Allen ditched Mia for Soon-Yi, Mia sent him a knife-skewered valentine.
▲ Sean Young allegedly had a mutilated voodoo doll delivered to James Woods' home.
▲ Kiefer Sutherland hired someone to fly over Julia Roberts' house and write "Julia Has Bird Legs" in the sky.*

Celebrities have learned that the tabloids themselves are great revenge tools. I've read countless interviews of newly

*Okay, so I made this one up. It could happen.

single actresses in which the phone rang mid-interview and the actress picked it up, cooed for a while, and then told the interviewer, "That was my new boyfriend, Mr. Perfect."

I myself have always found this tactic to be incredibly transparent, but evidently it works.

And what better way to spread rumors and stab your ex in the back than by getting your gibes into print? I'm thinking here of Burt Reynolds, who told *People* that Loni was "an underemployed actress suffering from low self-esteem who is not a good mother." And not only that, but during their five-year marriage, "she only cooked nine or eleven times, and it was all pasta."

And so in this chapter I have proven that the age-old maxim still holds true: "Living well is the best revenge only when your ex is miserable."

5

Hibernation

When the Going Gets Tough, the Tough Hide in Their Bedrooms

 AFTER HOURS of intense research,* I have determined that there are actually three kinds of post-breakup hibernation.

▲▲▲▲▲▲▲▲▲▲▲▲▲▲▲▲▲▲▲▲▲▲▲▲

Hibernation Type One: True Hibernation

The first is what I call True, or Bearlike, Hibernation, defined here as hibernation in which you run to your bedroom, dive under the covers, and refuse to come out except in cases of dire emergency (like when there's a fire or an

---

*Well, really, 45 minutes spent chewing my pencil and trying to think of something to write.

63

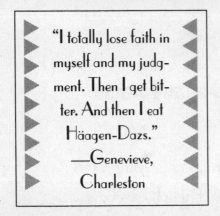

"I totally lose faith in myself and my judgment. Then I get bitter. And then I eat Häagen-Dazs."
—Genevieve, Charleston

earthquake, or you really have to pee).

For True Hibernation to be effective, you must (1) unplug your phone and/or your answering machine, (2) let your personal hygiene slide (no shaving, no showering, no trimming your toenails), and (3) gorge yourself on sweets until you earn the nickname "Rotunda, Queen of the Carbohydrates." After about three or four days, concerned friends will start pounding on your door till you answer. When you do, they'll say, "Are you okay? Are you depressed? My God—*you must weigh three hundred pounds! And you really stink, too!*"

Because of the weight gain involved, True Hibernation is most effective in small doses—say, over a three-day weekend. And it really only works for introverted, naturally depressed types, the kind of people who feel best about themselves when they're wallowing in their misery (you know who you are).

Writing this brings back fond memories of a particularly grueling post-breakup trauma I endured a while back. I think I must have hibernated for a whole year, coming out of my apartment only to get the mail and maybe go to work. The weekends were the worst. From Friday night to Monday morning, I'd just lie there in bed with my blinds drawn, surrounded by empty food wrappers, soggy Kleenex, and tattered copies of the *National Enquirer*. On Monday morning, I'd drag myself out of bed, shuffle through the refuse, take a

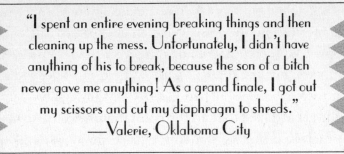

"I spent an entire evening breaking things and then cleaning up the mess. Unfortunately, I didn't have anything of his to break, because the son of a bitch never gave me anything! As a grand finale, I got out my scissors and cut my diaphragm to shreds."
—Valerie, Oklahoma City

shower, and then go off to work, shielding my eyes from the sunlight like some kind of vampire or mole.

What finally snapped me out of it was the alarming realization that I was becoming a Really Weird Person.

Yes, it's true: Too much time alone will make you strange. This is actually a proven scientific fact that I read somewhere. But I didn't need proof, because I learned it firsthand.

When you spend a lot of time alone, your mind tends to go off on strange tangents—and if you've just suffered a breakup, these tangents tend to be extremely negative. For example, once while I was hibernating, I read in the *Washington Post* (or maybe it was the *Weekly World News*) that scientists had just discovered a new type of algae called a dinoflagellate. Sounds tame enough, but—here's the kicker—dinoflagellates swell to 100 times their size *and* secrete a "deadly nerve toxin" when a fish (human? *me?!?*) swims by.

As I read this, my thoughts kind of ping-ponged from "Good Lord!" to "Fine! I'll just go to the beach, swim around, and dinoflagellate myself to death. Boy, will my ex be sorry *then!*"

Another time, I was reading a pharmaceutical newsletter* and found out that when researchers were testing a new cold medication, they discovered an unexpected side effect: People who took it had an orgasm every time they *sneezed*. Of course, my first thought was, "Where can I get some of that there medicine?" Then I started imagining how people would get addicted to it, to the point that they'd try to make themselves sneeze by standing outside in snowstorms until they caught cold, buying cats if they were allergic, spraying themselves with Calvin Klein Eternity, etc. Instead of having orgies, people would sit in a circle and pass around a pepper mill! Kleenex stock would skyrocket! No one would have sex anymore! Life as we know it would cease to exist!

During yet another post-breakup hibernation phase, I came across a statistic in *American Demographics* that said that being unmarried is more dangerous than having cancer. Before you start panicking, let me say that *American Demographics* gave no explanation for this statistic whatsoever. And yes, I was really pissed off about it, too.

In summary: Sequestering yourself for long periods of time can make you odd. If you're already odd, it will make you Really, Really Odd, to the point that you might start talking to your houseplants as if they were your ex-boyfriend, only more communicative. It's a natural mistake, but one that other people might frown upon, especially if you start doing it in public.

*Okay, so I was desperate.

▲▲▲▲▲▲▲▲▲▲▲▲▲▲▲▲▲▲▲▲▲▲▲▲▲

Hibernation Type Two:
New-You Hibernation

New-You Hibernation, also known as Susan Powter Hibernation, involves using your time alone to improve your mind, body, and/or spirit. This is actually pretty positive, so I don't know much about it. However, in the interests of ethical journalism (assuming that there still *is* such a thing), I interviewed a bunch of women who have used their post-breakup time to better themselves, giving themselves a veritable post-breakup *mind and body makeover*, as it were. Here's what they said:

▲ "After a breakup, I spend at least a month in my apartment doing the Buns of Steel workout, giving myself facials, and reading Proust. When I emerge, I look and feel fabulous. Bonus: My ex always wants me back at this point—and then I get to stomp on his little heart the way he stomped on mine."

▲ "I recommend that, while hibernating, you try something new that interests you—preferably something that your ex would hate. In the past, I've taken a class in papermaking, learned Hungarian, and even got a nose ring. I've found that if you change yourself in a positive way, it helps you get over the relationship. It enables you to say, 'I'm no longer the insecure person who dated that jerk. I've moved on.'"

▲ "After a breakup, I create a special Sunday 'hibernation

ritual' for myself. I take a bath, go to the market, get lots of fresh food, and make a fabulous dinner for myself—complete with candles and after-dinner liqueur. To really make it fun, I sometimes playact that my ex is with me. He had so many awful table habits: He'd start eating before I even sat down; he'd talk with his mouth full; he'd sit there with his arm around his plate and just shovel the food in. Visualizing this makes me realize how much nicer it is to be alone!"

▲ "I spend my post-breakup hibernation time reminding myself that I'm not a loser if there isn't a man in my life. I treat it as a period of self-discovery—a time to uncover the long-silent, long-neglected parts of my psyche."

▲ "My in-betweens with men are my most productive periods. I use the time to reevaluate my goals and plan how to achieve them. This helps me focus on the future, instead of on my current loneliness. To boost my motivation further, I read biographies of strong women who also did amazing things when they were between men."

▲ "I don't hibernate in my apartment. Instead, I make lots of outside commitments. I volunteer at the library, offer to babysit for friends, join a gym. Knowing that someone's depending on me to be somewhere helps me drag my butt off the couch and keeps me from feeling sorry for myself."

I would like to add that one of the best things about New-You Hibernation is that it gives you lots of time to ponder the important questions of life, such as

▲ "What will I do if Clairol discontinues my hair color?"

▲ "Aren't Rod Stewart and Ron Wood really the same person wearing two different wigs?"

▲ "If all my ex-boyfriends got into a bus and began traveling north at 60 miles an hour and I drove south at 75 miles an hour, how long would it take for me to have a nervous breakdown at the thought that they are all talking about me, assuming that they are?"

▲▲▲▲▲▲▲▲▲▲▲▲▲▲▲▲▲▲▲▲▲▲▲▲

Hibernation Type Three: Sexual Hibernation

I define Sexual Hibernation as hibernation in which you continue with life as usual, except that you don't have sex.

This is actually a tactic I know a lot about. After my last major breakup, I went through what I now call my Year-Long Dry Spell. Instead of dating, I cultivated close platonic friendships with some really great people of the opposite sex. This kept me from hating men as a species. In fact, it helped me genuinely *like* men again, and it showed me that there really are some nice guys out there—guys who liked me for who I was *inside* instead of for what I looked like *outside*.

I think every woman should have at least one man who's crazy about her who she's not sleeping with (and who she's not related to). But I have to warn you that some men can't handle platonic relationships. Some men only put up with them because their male ego has convinced them that sooner or later, you'll give in to your natural attraction to them and they'll get some nookie. In about ten years, they will suddenly realize that maybe, just maybe, they're *not* going to get some nookie. When that happens, they'll drop you like a hot potato and run off to Vegas with some bimbo named Bunny in a pathetic attempt to bolster their shaken masculinity. After a week with Bunny, they'll feel like themselves again, firm in the belief that they are Adonis and you were simply frigid.

Sexual dry spells are not for the faint of heart. For one thing, people who are happy without sex tend to make other people very nervous. They think *you're* thinking, "I am a superior being. You, on the other hand, are a rutting animal who can't control her own disgusting sexual urges."

I know this because whenever I was upset during my dry spell, male *and* female friends would try to get some of their power back by saying things like, "Boy, you really need to get laid," or, "Whatsa matter—not getting any?"

These comments sometimes made me huffy, but mostly I knew it was sour grapes: They were just jealous because I was, indeed, a superior being.

Another thing to remember about sexual dry spells is that just because you're not having sex doesn't mean you'll be able to stop *thinking* about sex. You will think about sex as much as you ever did. It's important that you don't try to bury these thoughts, because if you do, they'll manifest themselves in your dreams, usually in a very disturbing way. I know, because during my period of celibacy I dreamt that I had sex with Kermit the Frog—and that it was *good!*

▲▲▲

For these reasons and more, hibernation requires courage. But the rewards are many. Not only does hibernation—and the introspection that goes with it—help you feel better about yourself, it keeps you, in the words of one woman, "from repeating the same relationship mistakes with a changing cast of characters."

6

The Rebound Date

THE FLIP SIDE of sexual hibernation is the dreaded and much-maligned rebound date. Though rebound dating is not a tactic that has worked for me personally, enough women swear by it that I feel obliged to present it as an option. Some of the pluses:

▲ It keeps you from feeling lonely.

▲ It boosts self-esteem and helps you feel attractive.

▲ Having sex with a rebound date may improve your health.* According to one article, sex "has unheralded healing powers. It builds up the immune system, relieving chronic pain, stiffness, and migraines and preventing heart disease." As proof of these wonderful benefits, the article cites a study which found that "golden hamsters allowed to copulate freely remained healthy even after being injected with cancer-causing chemicals. Their celibate companions sickened and died from the

*Of *course* I mean safe sex, you silly fool.

> "If you're the rebound-dating type, don't try to suppress it. A biologist friend of mine thought that isolating herself from men would keep her from dating creeps on the rebound, so she moved to the Florida swamps to count birds. She thought she'd be safe, since there were literally no men for 200 miles. The only guy she saw was the pilot of the prop-engine plane that flew in occasionally to drop supplies. This guy was a chain-smoking Swedish gun collector who barely spoke English; he was also an emotionally abusive liar, a thief, and a cheat. Guess what? My friend ended up buying a mobile home and moving in with him."
> —Kyra, Louisville

same injections." And we all know how much humans have in common with hamsters.†

▲ If the sex is good, it will help you get over any bad sexual experiences you might have had with your ex. I'm thinking here of the woman who, after having sex with her rebound date, suddenly realized that her ex's hook-shaped penis was *not* normal, as he had claimed.

▲ Your rebound date may turn out to be your One True Love. Yes, friends will tell you that this is impossible. They'll also tell you that it would be pretty darn impossible to step on an unwrapped ice cream bar while walking down a deserted New York street in the dead of winter. But this has happened to me. Besides, we all know of

†Nothing.

guys who broke up with their longtime girlfriends, then turned around and married the next girl they dated after knowing her for two weeks. If it works for them, it can work for you.

In summary, rebound dating can divert your attention from your relationship woes. As one woman put it, "My mom always told me that the best way to get over a man is with another man, and I have found this to be 99.5 percent accurate. The new person serves as a distraction, something to immerse yourself in to forget your ex."

The key word here, of course, is "some*thing*." When you date on the rebound, you are treating another human being (or, in this case, a guy) as a thing, an object, a tool to aid in your own healing, without regard for this human being's feelings.

Sounds great! you're probably thinking. But let me warn you: Rebound dating is also fraught with pitfalls, such as:

▲ While out on your rebound date, you may see your ex with *his* rebound date. Then one of three things will happen:

1. You will feel so upset that you will run home and cry yourself to sleep.
2. You will feel so upset that you will run home and have sex with your rebound date even if you don't want to, just to piss off your ex. *Then* you will cry yourself to sleep.
3. You and your ex will begin a Rebound-Dating Competition, with both of you battling over

who can date the most and best-looking people. Eventually, your ex will date Cindy Crawford, and you will have to kill yourself.*

▲ Your rebound date might fall in love with you, and then you'll never be able to get rid of him. "Whenever I date on the rebound, I get stuck with these Klingons I don't even want," complained one woman. "At first, it's really nice to have someone worship you, but then it starts to make you sick. One guy was always saying things like, 'Can I watch you put your makeup on?' 'Would you like something else now?' It got to the point that I had to have five shots of Jack Daniel's before I could even look at him." Another woman's rebound date told her that he loved her after only a week. "I had to pretend I was asleep," she said.

▲ You might fall in love with your rebound date, but he won't marry you because he *knows* he's a rebound date. Yes, men now know all about the rebound syndrome. And we have only ourselves to blame, because we're the ones who forced them to take us to see *When Harry Met Sally*, a movie that revealed many heretofore unknown female dating secrets.

▲ The men you date on the rebound may actually be worse than your ex. This seems as good a place as any to mention a recent and very important guppy study. Scientists have discovered that male guppies watch to see who female guppies reject, then they hang around the rejects, the idea being that they'll seem more attractive in com-

*We do, after all, live in an era in which even kite flying has become competitive, as evidenced by the new sport, *power* kite flying.

parison with these "guppy nerds," if you will. Actual scientist quote: "Even fish with brains as small as pinheads are capable of surprisingly sophisticated social behavior." It only follows, then, that *guys* might be onto this trick, too. So the next time you go to a singles bar, you—much like the female guppy—will have to ask yourself some hard questions, namely, *Which ones are the nerds?*

If you'd like further proof that there are guys out there who are worse than your ex—or if reading about someone else's awful experiences makes you feel better about yourself—consider the following sad but true stories of rebound dates gone bad:

▲ One woman's rebound date didn't show, so she went over to his house to see what happened. When she knocked on his door, her "date" suddenly jerked it open and then sprayed her with a fire extinguisher for a full two minutes. Then he said, "Oh, sorry, I thought you were someone else."

▲ Another woman met a nice-looking guy who asked her if she'd like to go out to dinner sometime. She said, "Sure, here's my card." The next day at work, the woman received several psychotic phone calls from the guy's jealous girlfriend. She explained to the girlfriend that the guy had only asked her to dinner and that she didn't even know him, but the girlfriend wouldn't listen. Finally the woman stopped answering her phone. When it rang again, her *boss* answered it, and the jealous girlfriend told the boss that the woman was a "f—ing slut" and that, in the future, the boss should be more discriminating when hiring employees.

▲ One woman's date asked her up for coffee afterward, and she, poor naïve thing, said okay. When he started putting the moves on her, she said, "I'm sorry. I'm not ready for sex. I just broke up with my boyfriend." Her date replied: "Oh. I understand." After a brief pause, he said, "Well, how about just giving me a blow job?" When she said no, he threw her out of the apartment and slammed the door in her face.

▲ Another woman rebound-dated a guy who never called when he said he was going to; she'd run into him on the street and he'd say, "What a coincidence! I almost called you, but something came up." Being no dummy, she stopped dating him. Months later, she saw him at a party, and he said, "What a coincidence! I was going to call you, but something came up!" And she replied, "What a coincidence! I was going to hang up on you!"

▲ One woman's rebound date slept over. When she made breakfast for him the next day, he screamed, "My God! This is awful! There's a little piece of eggshell in the scrambled eggs, and you didn't put the toast on the right side of the plate! *Aargh!*" He stormed out, never to be seen again.

▲ Another woman stopped at the grocery store with her date to pick up some snacks. He said he wanted some nuts, so he went to one of those pay-by-the-pound nut things. A few minutes later, she caught him scooping cashews into his peanuts so he could get them at the cheaper peanut price.

▲ While on a dinner date, one woman went to the bathroom; when she came back she saw three tiny pieces of paper on the table, "folded so small they looked like lint." Her date quickly put them in his pocket and said, "Oh, these are just phone numbers I'm holding for my friend."

▲ One woman's rebound date turned out to be a chronic masturbator. He masturbated five times a day, whether or not she was there. She stopped seeing him when he . . .

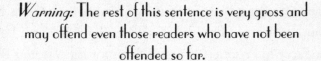

Warning: The rest of this sentence is very gross and may offend even those readers who have not been offended so far.

. . . had a wet dream on her back one night.

Bad rebound dates like these will make it hard for you to like men as people. They'll make you think that men love to prey on vulnerable single women, which will make you feel bitter. They'll make you think that you've heard more lines than Lee Strasberg, the famous drama coach, which will make you feel jaded. Bitter and jaded aren't good. The only woman who's ever pulled them off with aplomb was Dorothy Parker, and she was an alcoholic. Plus, she's dead.

If, after these dire warnings, you decide to attempt the rebound date, you should know that some guys make better rebound dates than others. The general rule: Men who would make awful boyfriends make the best rebound dates. Some examples:

▲ Musicians, actors, pro athletes—any guy with an entourage of screaming fans. *Pros:* Your friends will be impressed. *They make bad boyfriends because:* They'll sleep with every one of their screaming fans until they turn sixty. Then they'll die.

▲ Monks (one woman dated a Gregorian monk who looked exactly like Gary on *Thirtysomething*). *Pros:* Respectful, quiet, good chanters. *They make bad boyfriends because:* Well, they're *monks*.

▲ Men who aren't going to be around long for reasons that have nothing to do with you. This list includes: ▲ Men on Vacation (yours or theirs), ▲ Sailors on Shore Leave, ▲ Escaped Prisoners, ▲ Candidates for the Witness Relocation Program, ▲ Men in Hotel Bars, and the ever-dependable ▲ Foreign Men. Of the latter, one woman said: "The best rebound date I ever had was this French guy named Jacques. He came to town every six months or so. The only English words he knew were, 'Leila, it's Jacques. I arrive.'" Another woman dated a married guy in Gorky Park, Russia, *before* the Iron Curtain fell. (How's *that* for fear of commitment?) *Pros:* Lots of fun with no strings attached. *They make bad boyfriends because:* They tend to disappear off the face of the earth.

Tip: If you date a guy who's not going to be around for long, give him a fake name and address. Otherwise, you might end up like one woman, who started getting mail like this: "I told all my friends in driver's ed about you and how good-looking you are and how you should be a model, but no one believed me. Please send me a picture, because otherwise I won't be able to convince them that you really exist."

Other rebound dates aren't so black-and-white. The following clip-and-save list should help you make an informed decision, thereby ensuring that your rebound date experience is as pleasant as possible.

▲▲▲▲▲▲▲▲▲▲▲▲▲▲▲▲▲▲▲▲▲▲▲▲▲

The E-Mail Date

Motto: "On the Internet, all dates are blind."

Pros:

▲ You can date a guy without ever seeing him or smelling his breath.

▲ You can actually get to know the guy intimately *before* you give him your name and phone number.

▲ You can "date" while sitting at your computer with mayonnaise on your face, big pink rollers in your hair, and a pint of Cherry Garcia ice cream by your side, and he'll be none the wiser.

▲ You can pretend to be Cindy Crawford.

Cons:

▲ Not being able to see you won't prevent some men from being sexist pigs. The first time one woman logged on to America Online, she got the immediate message, "Will you chain me up and make me kiss your feet?" *Tip:* Choosing a gender-neutral screen name such as The

Terminator may spare you from the weirdos who automatically target women.

▲ The guy with the screen name HanSome, with whom you've shared several dirty secrets, may turn out to be a fourteen-year-old with a severe case of acne and a very angry mother.

▲ When you get your phone bill, you might have a heart attack. Most online services cost about $3.60 an hour. If you surf the Net for two hours a night, that works out to $216 a month. And that's on top of the charges for all those hang-up calls you've been making to your ex in spite of my advice.

▲▲▲▲▲▲▲▲▲▲▲▲▲▲▲▲▲▲▲▲▲▲▲▲

The UPS Man

Motto: "He comes every day." (Ahem.)

Pros:

▲ He's dependable.
▲ He has a job.
▲ He wears a sexy uniform.

Cons:

▲ You will spend millions of dollars ordering things you don't need just so he'll come over.
▲ You will get jealous of his other so-called clients.

▲▲▲▲▲▲▲▲▲▲▲▲▲▲▲▲▲▲▲▲▲▲▲▲

The Singles-Bar Date

Motto: "After twenty cocktails, even the barstool looks attractive."

Pros:

▲ Free drinks.
▲ You will feel so hip, so liberated, so Charlie.

Con:

▲ You might wake up in the morning and find yourself sleeping with a barstool.

▲▲▲▲▲▲▲▲▲▲▲▲▲▲▲▲▲▲▲▲▲▲▲▲

The Slimeball-You-Wouldn't-Be-Caught-Dead-with-If-You-Weren't-Feeling-Desperate Date

Motto: "Any date is better than sitting at home with Grandma."

Pro:

▲ Will give you renewed appreciation for Grandma.

Con:

▲ Murphy's Law says that your ex will see you with this doofus and have a good laugh at your expense.

▲▲▲▲▲▲▲▲▲▲▲▲▲▲▲▲▲▲▲▲▲▲▲▲▲

The Ex-Boyfriend's Brother/Best Friend Date

Motto: "He who laughs last has the best revenge, thereby killing two birds with one stone."

Pros:

▲ Will make your ex furious.
▲ May ruin his relationship with said brother/best friend, making him a very unhappy person.

Con:

▲ Only works for characters on *Melrose Place* and *Beverly Hills 90210.*

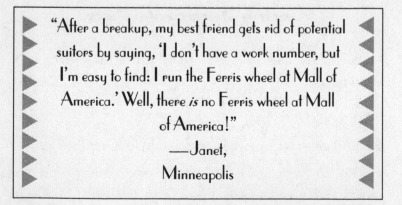

"After a breakup, my best friend gets rid of potential suitors by saying, 'I don't have a work number, but I'm easy to find: I run the Ferris wheel at Mall of America.' Well, there *is* no Ferris wheel at Mall of America!"
—Janet,
Minneapolis

7

Movies, Books, and Songs You Should Seek Out During This Phase

(And Those You Should Avoid Like the Plague)

MOVIES, BOOKS, AND songs are great distractions after a breakup, provided you choose the right ones. So I racked my brains and came up with the following suggestions as a guideline. (Am I great, or what?)

▲▲▲▲▲▲▲▲▲▲▲▲▲▲▲▲▲▲▲▲▲▲▲▲

Movies to See

▲ Woody Allen movies, because they reinforce the idea that relationships are hell and make you happy to be single. Plus, they make you laugh.
▲ Men Are Real Idiots movies: *The Jerk, Dumb and Dumber, Billy Madison, Look Who's Stupid Now* (or what-

ever Jim Carrey's latest movie is called), *Greystoke: The Legend of Tarzan* (which illustrates the folly of teaching men to speak).

▲ Any movies that you loved and your ex hated, because watching them reinforces the idea that you were totally wrong for each other. (I realize that this bit of advice may cause a run on rentals of *The Piano*, but I'm willing to take that chance.)

▲ Bitches from Hell movies, such as *She-Devil* (Roseanne on a rampage), *Out Cold* (Teri Garr puts philandering husband on ice), *Girlfriend from Hell* (woman becomes life—and death—of the party after she is possessed by the Devil), and *Faster Pussycat! Kill! Kill!* (gorgeous woman beats the crap out of men while regaling us with fabulous B-movie dialogue. Example: *Man unknowingly on verge of death:* "Do you have a point?" *Woman on verge of kicking his butt:* "Yeah, a point of no return—and you've passed it!")

▲ Men Are Pigs movies: *Porky's* springs to mind as an especially porcine example, along with *Animal House* ('nuff said) and *Scent of a Woman* (moral: Even blind men can be sexist). I could go on, but the list is endless and this is just a measly paperback.

▲ Escape movies, including *Shirley Valentine* (bored housewife goes to Greece), *Enchanted April* (bored housewives go to Italy), *Now, Voyager* (Bette Davis finds herself abroad—in more ways than one), and *Room with a View* (male frontal nudity).

And speaking of male frontal nudity, I would like to make special mention of the Learning Channel show *The*

Operation. This is a great venue for indulging any castration fantasies you may have, because it often shows vasectomies in progress.

▲▲▲▲▲▲▲▲▲▲▲▲▲▲▲▲▲▲▲▲▲▲▲▲▲

Movies to Avoid

▲ Any movie that you saw with your ex or that reminds you of him in any way.
▲ Sappy romances or any movie in which a man and a woman have sex and are still together at the end.
▲ Movies with gratuitous sex scenes. (Unfortunately, this limits you to war films, kung fu movies, or *Dumbo*.)

▲▲▲▲▲▲▲▲▲▲▲▲▲▲▲▲▲▲▲▲▲▲▲▲▲

Books to Read

▲ Any book that makes your problems seem small by comparison (*The Diary of Anne Frank*, *A Tree Grows in Brooklyn*, *The Autobiography of Helen Keller*).
▲ Biographies about strong women.
▲ *The Clan of the Cave Bear* series: Set in prehistoric times, this series of novels focuses on a strong Cro-Magnon woman who must literally deal with a bunch of Neanderthals. (I'm sure we can *all* relate.)
▲ Escapist books: Anything that gets your mind off your ex for more than five minutes, including novels by Agatha Christie, John Grisham, and Stephen King.

▲ Books that confirm that you're not alone in your relationship hell. Cynthia Heimel's books *Get Your Tongue Out of My Mouth, I'm Kissing You Goodbye* and *If You Can't Live Without Me, Why Aren't You Dead Yet?* are two great and funny choices.

▲▲▲▲▲▲▲▲▲▲▲▲▲▲▲▲▲▲▲▲▲▲▲▲

Books to Avoid

Romance novels: At this stage, they'll only depress you and make you miss your ex. Plus, they may make you idolize Fabio, and we *don't want that!*

▲▲▲▲▲▲▲▲▲▲▲▲▲▲▲▲▲▲▲▲▲▲▲▲

Music to Listen To

Basically, just about any attitude song is good, especially if it's sung by a woman. There are lots of these out there, a few examples being the TLC song "Bad By Myself," En Vogue's "My Lovin' (You're Never Gonna Get It)," Jody Watley's "Looking for a New Love," Madonna's "Bye Bye, Baby," Monie Love's self-explanatory "I Just Don't Give a Damn," and the Voodoo Queens' song "I'm Not Bitter, I Just Wish You Were Dead."

After my last breakup, I even went so far as to make a breakup tape for myself, and I listened to it whenever I started missing my ex. You may want to do the same.

▲▲▲▲▲▲▲▲▲▲▲▲▲▲▲▲▲▲▲▲▲▲▲▲

Music to Avoid

Repeat after me: No country music. No sad love songs. No *happy* love songs. And absolutely, positively *no blues!* If you think that listening to music like this will make you feel better, think again. It will more likely send you flying into the kitchen for a knife with which to slit your wrists—or flying to the corner bar, where you'll drown your sorrows in Jack Daniel's, puke on your shoes, and go home with some guy who chews tobacco. (At least, this is what I've *heard* will happen.)

You should obviously avoid listening to "your song," and I suggest you also avoid "Memories," "The Way We Were," "Feelings," and "Yesterday," not to mention "Endless Love," "Always and Forever," and anything by Cole Porter or Patsy Cline. Oh—and Whitney Houston, too, especially her song "I Have Nothing (If I Don't Have You)." Attention, Whitney: Run, don't walk, to your nearest support group for codependents.

Speaking of codependents, I also have a few choice words for the person who wrote "How Am I Supposed to Live Without You?"

Q: How am I supposed to live without you, now that I've been loving you so long? How am I supposed to carry on when all that I was living for is gone?
A: Easy.

As you can see, songs are rife with emotional grenades at this stage, so it's probably best to turn off your radio altogether for these first few months. And don't forget to turn your clock radio to "alarm." If you have the misfortune to wake up to a song that reminds you of your ex, *you won't be able to get it out of your head all day and you will slowly be driven insane.*

Part Two

Five to Eight Months Later:

You're Not Over Him Yet?

5 Signs That You Haven't
Made a Clean Break

▲ You spend so much time watching sappy made-for-TV movies that you have bedsores on your butt.

▲ Whenever you see your ex with a strange* woman you start to have an asthma attack—and you don't even have asthma.

▲ Your ex's picture still graces your dart board.

▲ You hate every guy who has the same first name as your ex, even if your ex's first name was Keanu, Harrison, or John-John.

▲ Your phone conversations with your friends all go something like this:

YOU: Shirley! I'm so glad I caught you in person! Didn't you get my messages? I left about twenty.

SHIRLEY: Oh, uh, yeah, I've just been so busy lately. . . .

YOU (interrupting her): You're not going to *believe* what happened. Last night I was driving past McDonald's and I saw Derek inside with a bunch of his friends and—get *this*—he was *talking and laughing.* Can you believe that scumbag? What *nerve!* After all I did for him! I mean, to be talking *and* laughing. It was so obvious that he was just pretending to be happy. Don't you think?

SHIRLEY: Um, well . . . gosh! Look at the time! I've got to go. I'm expecting an important call from my . . . optician! Yes, my optician will be calling any minute now with some very important news! Gotta go! Bye! (*Click*)

*That is, unfamiliar.

8

Self-Help Books

Should You Read Them? Avoid Them? Use Them for Firewood?

OKAY, so four months have passed and you're still feeling miserable about the breakup. I regret to inform you that this can only mean one thing: Something is Really Wrong with you.

Just kidding. As we learned in Chapter 2, it can take years, even decades, to get over an ex, even if your entire relationship consisted of a single lunch date at Wendy's.

You might not believe this. You might think that something really *is* wrong with you. One woman told me, "After a breakup, I inevitably think that if I had just acted differently, the relationship wouldn't have ended the way it did. That if I could only change myself, I'd never have a bad relationship again."

It's this kind of reasoning that sends women running for the self-help section after a breakup, as if books like *Was It Love or Was It Memorex?*; *I'm OK, You're a Big Asshole*; or

Goodbye to Guilt: Releasing Shame and Anger Through Acts of Extreme Violence could fix their relationship problems.

It's very important that you resist this self-help impulse, at least for a few months. Why? Because though the desire to change can be quite admirable, it overlooks one important fact: Relationships involve *two* people. You could become as sickeningly sweet as Melanie in *Gone With the Wind* and *still* have a bad relationship if you hooked up with the wrong guy.

Here are three more good reasons to avoid self-help books for the time being:

1. They'll make your eyes glaze over. Self-help books tend to be very bad reads. This is because they're written by psychologists and therapists, people who love to throw around phrases like "empirical data" and "paranoid schizophrenic." (They also like to use the word "impact" as a verb, one of my personal pet peeves.) Plus, psychologists tend to drone on and on. You don't believe me? Here's an actual quote from a self-help book that shall remain nameless:

    Some people are tall, others short; some are thin, others fat; some are energetic, others phlegmatic.* Some are born colicky and are irritable and highly strung; others are born calm and cheerful; some are bright, lively and talented; others dull.

    Some are poor, others well-to-do. Some have parents who are divorced or have lost one or both parents

*Gross.

at an early age. Some parents can be cold and demanding, indifferent, insensitive, or even abusive, and other parents are warm, intelligent, and nurturing.

To this I would add: "Some state the obvious to the point that they become extremely annoying and you want to throw their book out the window; others don't."

The problem with boring books is that they make your mind wander, and while your mind is wandering, thoughts of your ex may wriggle their way to the forefront. We don't want that, now, do we?

2. No matter what psychological disorder the book focuses on, you'll become convinced you have it. Every author wants her book to sell, and self-help authors are no different. Therefore, the symptoms of these disorders *du jour* are often very broad, the idea being that the more people the book applies to, the more money it will make. Here, for example, are some actual "symptoms" described in various self-help books:

▲ You feel low self-esteem when you're alone and not involved with a loved one.
▲ You feel a sense of desolation.
▲ You have a fear of loneliness.
▲ You have picked the wrong mate.
▲ No matter how intense your feelings for your love object, you eventually find yourself losing the person.

Does one or more of these apply to you? Congratulations! You're codependent/a love slave/a borderline personality.

(In case you hadn't noticed, I'd like to point out that every single one of these statements will apply to anyone who's recently gone through a breakup.)

Remember: The advice in self-help books can be very objective. In extreme cases, the author *may be making it up entirely*. I know this from experience.

3.   Trying to fix psychological problems while you're in the midst of despair is like trying to find your glasses when you don't have them on. How are you supposed to accurately analyze your psyche when you're sunk in self-loathing? How are you supposed to "think positive" when you feel like killing yourself, your ex, your paper boy? Let's face it: When you're feeling vulnerable and unattractive (as many women do after a breakup), most self-help advice just seems ludicrous. At worst, it might incite homicidal rages.

To illustrate this point, I've lifted actual self-help exercises from several published books. You will first read these exercises as they appeared in print. Then you will read *my* take on them. Let's begin.

SELF-HELP EXERCISE #1: "Mirror Love." "Go to a mirror. Look deep into your eyes. Tell yourself 'I love you.'"

Supposedly you *will* come to love yourself if you do this exercise often enough. I wouldn't know. Every time I attempted it, I noticed some new wrinkle and could only focus on that. So I asked a friend to try it. "No way," she said. "Knowing me, I'd start feeling myself up. Then I'd get too serious about myself, and that would bring up my fear of intimacy. Eventually, I'd have to break up with my-self."

Tip: If you do try this exercise, make sure your shades are drawn. Otherwise your neighbors might start calling you That Weirdo Next Door Who Talks to Her Reflection.

SELF-HELP EXERCISE #2: "Happy Thoughts." "In spite of your belief, you are not *totally* sad. One counterintuitive way to encourage inklings of happiness is to focus on trying *not* to be happy. Take a few minutes to push all happiness out of your mind. Definitely do not let any happy memory, sensation, or plan intrude. Most people cannot do so. This experiment can get you in touch with your innate capacity for joy."

My initial response to this exercise: "Screw you." (Maybe I'm strange, but when I'm depressed, I can go for days, even *months* without having a happy thought.) Unexpected result: This exercise helped me get in touch with my innate hatred for happy people.

SELF-HELP EXERCISE #3: "Tell Your Story to Others." Many books recommend joining groups like "Mending Ripped Seams: A Workshop for Women with Broken Hearts." (I'm not making this group up—but I wish I were.)

> "When my ex moved out, I didn't even cry. I was excited to have my space to myself again. He had a gun rack that did *not* go with my decor; I was very happy to see it go."
> —Dalena, Los Angeles

Group therapy theory holds that talking to people who've gone through similar experiences will help you get over your problems. But I think that therapy groups can be damaging, because when you join one, your "problem" becomes the most important thing about you. Instead of seeing yourself as a vital, attractive woman who's just having a hard time meeting the right guy, you'll see yourself as an emotionally damaged woman who has trouble with relationships. So you will continue dating men who are wrong for you, because you'll think you can't do any better.

Instead of telling your story to a group of fellow sufferers, I suggest that you tell it, in extreme detail, (1) on a huge billboard overlooking your ex's house, or (2) by yelling it at the top of your lungs while standing outside your ex's new girlfriend's house. I guarantee you'll feel much, much better.

SELF-HELP EXERCISE #4: "Plan Your Week." The idea: Creating a routine and sticking to it is comforting, and it keeps you from wasting much-needed post-breakup energy on trivial decisions.

The following post-breakup routine was recommended to me by several women: (1) Cry. (2) Eat. (3) Sleep. (4) Eat. (5) Put self down. (6) Cry. (7) Sleep. (8) Feel fat. (9) Eat. (10) Repeat steps 1–9.

SELF-HELP EXERCISE #5: "Create a Weekly Ritual." "Make up a weekly ritual that honors you for growing. It could be as simple as making yourself a fresh fruit salad on Saturday mornings, looking at the sky on Sunday nights, and making a wish or lighting a candle."

Suggested ritual: Sending hate mail to a different self-help author each week.

SELF-HELP EXERCISE #6: "Send Your Personal Critic on a Vacation." Upon reading this suggestion, I immediately called my mother and asked her if she'd like to take a solo trip to the Bahamas. Then I realized that the book had been talking about my *inner* critic. Silly me.

> "After the breakup I did a kind of voodoo ritual, using the *Star Wars* figurine he'd given me. I set it in the middle of the table, surrounded it with two kinds of incense, and prayed."
> —Lis, New York

SELF-HELP EXERCISE #7: "Learn to Make Something." "After a breakup you will have lots of spare time. This is a great opportunity to make something you've thought about but have never gotten around to learning about."

Great. Which should I learn to make first—a noose or a letter bomb?

SELF-HELP EXERCISE #8: "Write a Lost-and-Found Ad." "If you were to place an ad in the lost-and-found section of your local newspaper, what would you write about your losses? For example: 'Lost: Belief in people. Belief in justice. On Friday, March 7. If you have found them, please call.'"

A better idea: Place a classified ad in the Sunday *Times*. For example: "Lost:_____ *(ex's name here)*. Cried at *Terms of Endearment*. Loves to play hooky from his job

> "My ex was a carpenter and had done lots of touch-ups in my apartment. The problem was, he used glossy paint to touch up the matte walls. That was my first clue I was dealing with a real idiot. So the first thing I did after he left was repaint the house."
> —Petra, Los Angeles

at_____(company name here). Cheated on me with his best friend's fiancée; best friend still doesn't know. If found, don't call. Am happier without him."

SELF-HELP EXERCISE #9: "Give Yourself a Break."

"Many people feel overwhelmed by demands on their time and resources just when they need more of both to work on forgiving. In this exercise, write down all the demands that take away from your healing process." (My response: Reading this self-help book and making this dumb list.)

"In a corresponding list, write down any methods you could use to unburden yourself of these demands." (Throwing this self-help book away.)

SELF-HELP EXERCISE #10: "Photo Blame."

"Find a picture of the person who hurt you. In a place where you feel comfortable talking to a picture, tell the picture you think he hurt you intentionally. Tell it how angry you are. Explain exactly what the person did to you. Say, 'It's your fault. I did not deserve this.' How did you feel afterward?" (Stupid.)

SELF-HELP EXERCISE #11: "Write a Short History of Your Relationship." "Here are some questions to get you started. Number one: What were the most significant positive experiences in the relationship?" (The day we broke up.) "Number two: What did each of you do to make the relationship work?" (Me, everything; him, nothing.) "Number three: In what ways has this relationship added to your life?" (It gave me renewed appreciation for Puffs Plus with Aloe.) "Number four: What did this relationship teach you about relationships in general?" (They really suck.)

SELF-HELP EXERCISE #12: "Visualization." "Breathe deeply. Now begin to fill your body with light. Feel how each cell and each pore and each bone begins to respond to the light. Allow your body to *become* the light."

Allow yourself to run to the bathroom and throw up because this exercise is so sickening. (*Note:* One book actually recommended a *Dumpster visualization exercise* in which you visualize the unwanted parts of yourself leaving your body and being gobbled up by a huge, unsightly garbage can. When I tried it, I just kept picturing myself throwing my ex's dead body away. This was actually pretty effective.)

SELF-HELP EXERCISE #13: "The Balloon Exercise." "Make a list of the lingering debts you still feel your injurer owes you. Buy some helium-filled balloons. On each, write the items on your list with a Magic Marker. If you have a spot where you are reminded of your injurer, go there with your balloons. Imagine that the balloons with debts are the last remaining connections you have with your injurer. When you're ready, release your hold on the balloons one by one."

This exercise is bad for the environment, because balloons usually end up in water, where they choke unsuspecting wildlife. A better balloon exercise: Make a list of the lingering debts you still feel your injurer owes you. Buy a balloon. Put the list inside. Go to the roof of your ex's apartment building. Fill the balloon with water. When your ex comes out, drop the balloon on his head.

Okay, now that I've come down so hard on self-help books, I should probably say that a few of their suggestions actually *are* helpful.

For instance, I really like *affirmations*—those positive statements that help you feel better about yourself. For maximum effectiveness, you should always word these statements as if they're already true. ("I'd feel wonderful if my ex's penis would fall off" versus "My ex's penis has fallen off, and I feel wonderful.")

Here are some other post-breakup affirmations for you to try:

▲ "I am happy without my ex."
▲ "I am attractive, smart, and healthy."
▲ "I am dating the entire Dallas Cowboys football team."
▲ "The entire Dallas Cowboys football team is stepping on my ex's face."

I also like the coping strategy called "distancing and dehumanizing," though I don't remember if the self-help books were for it or against it. Anyway, this tactic involves numbing yourself by viewing your ex as the enemy. The easiest way to do this is by "renaming your ex." Inform your friends that from now on, your ex will be referred to as The Idiot, or, simply, Asshole. Or something really specific and disgusting, like Scuzzy Two-Inch Toenails or Chia Back.

According to the experts, using belittling slurs like these will eventually cause you to think of your ex as "less than human" (the dehumanizing part), after which you won't care about him anymore (the distancing part). When this happens, you'll be over your ex.

I'm especially fond of the popular post-breakup recommendation of "writing a letter to your ex." This is cathartic whether or not you mail it, because putting your feelings on paper helps you see things objectively. There's just one caveat: Writing down your ex's transgressions also makes them fresher in your mind; this may fan the flames of your anger even further. Therefore, it might be wise to wait a few months before mailing your missile, er, missive.

Here, for example, is the letter you'd write immediately after the breakup:

Dear Ex:

I HATE YOU! DIE! DIE, YOU ROTTEN SCUMBAG!

Now, the letter you'd write six months later:

Dear Ex:

In the months since our breakup, I've calmed down enough to realize that not everything was your fault. Okay, so you wrecked my truck, skipped out on the rent, and stuck me with a $1,000 phone bill for the calls you made to that sex line. I now see that I'm partially responsible for what happened. By not immediately kicking you out of my apartment and out of my life, I was subtly condoning your behavior. I think I did this because I saw you as I wished you were (i.e., a normal person) instead of seeing you as you really are (i.e., a slimy leech with virtually no good points). In closing, I'd like to say that I forgive you, I wish you a happy life, and if you ever contact me again I'm going to call the cops.

See the difference?

Tips: ▲ Don't Xerox the letter. If you can't remember exactly what you said, you won't feel guilty about it later. ▲ If you feel you should at least *pretend* to apologize, use the immortal words of Senator Bob Packwood, who, after being accused of sexually harassing at least a dozen women during his tenure in Congress, said: "I'm apologizing for the conduct that it was alleged that I did."

It's entirely possible that composing a letter to your ex will be too much for your poor nerves at this point. Just in case, I've drawn up a post-breakup form letter, specially designed to keep you from getting all hysterical and saying nasty things you might regret. To use, simply check off the phrases that apply and send it to your ex.

▲▲▲▲▲▲▲▲▲▲▲▲▲▲▲▲▲▲▲▲▲▲▲▲

Elizabeth Kuster's Fabulous Post-Breakup Form Letter

Dear_____: (*ex's name here*)

You are too __immature __self-absorbed __flatulent for me. You make me want to __become a nun __become a lesbian __throw up. I __have changed __have changed the locks __am pregnant with someone else's child and I'm not sure whose. I can't stand the way you __chew your toenails __salt your food __sound like Mr. Ed when you laugh.

Our relationship was __like something out of *The Twilight Zone* __like something out of *Friday the 13th* __a mistake of global proportions. I felt like I was sleeping with __my father __George Burns __On second thought, George Burns would be better in bed. I wish you would __leave me alone __leave the country __leave polka dancing to the professionals.

I hope you get over your unnatural obsession with your __drastic hair loss __love handles __butt pimples. I feel __sorry for your mother __sorry for your next girlfriend __glad I don't have to feign interest in your beer can collection anymore.

Sincerely, _____ (*your name here*)

P.S. I hate your __cat __best friend __brother, too.

P.P.S. The __Lakers __Cowboys __Yankees *really suck.*

Should you have a sudden attack of conscience after mailing this letter, remember that hate mail is not a new concept. A few years ago, archaeologists found a letter written on birchbark sometime around the year 1100. In the letter (which was torn into three pieces), a woman wrote, "What is the evil you hold against me? Even if I hurt you thoughtlessly, if you will begin mocking me, let God judge you."

The letter was signed "Shirley MacLaine." (Ha ha.)

To summarize this chapter, I'd like to repeat that using self-help books to analyze yourself after a breakup can be very risky. However, if you feel you *must* consult a self-help book, do what one wise woman did: "I bought *Smart Women, Foolish Choices* and underlined all the parts that described my ex. Then I mailed it to him. It made me feel *tons* better."

9

Some Stuff About Stuff

He's Gone, So Why's His Ratty Bathrobe Still Hanging in Your Closet?

AT SOME POINT after the breakup, you are going to have to deal with the problems of stuff. By "stuff," I mean all of the debris that serves as a concrete reminder of your ex—the flotsam and jetsam of your relationship.

Post-breakup stuff comes in many forms, including:

▲ The stuff he left at your house because he either forgot about it or didn't have time to grab it before you threw him out of the apartment
▲ The stuff you left at his house (ditto)
▲ All of the gifts he bought you during the relationship, from the designerlike perfume to the faux diamond earrings
▲ Any joint purchases you may have made (the recliner, the stereo, the "ribbed for her pleasure" condoms)

> "He had a file folder called 'Nancy' in his filing cabinet at work, filled with all the photos, cards, and letters I sent him. When I knew it was over, I went to his office and tried to take it. We got into a big shoving match; he won. His new girlfriend is probably looking through that folder right now."
> —Nancy, New York

▲ The Paper Trail of Love: letters, ticket stubs, journal entries, photos, the receipt they gave you when you paid his bail, etc.

Each type of post-breakup stuff must be handled differently, depending on how you feel about it. Some things you'll give back to your ex. Some you'll throw away. Some you'll stomp on, again and again, until it forms a sort of paste. And some you'll keep, either because it brings back particularly good memories or because you might be able to use it for blackmail later on.

Dealing with post-breakup stuff can be kind of tricky. Do it too soon—or too rashly—and you'll live to regret it. Put it off too long, and the stuff will go all Stephen King on you: It will meld together into a huge, pulsating blob, attach itself to your brain, and turn you into a drooling creature incapable of interacting with other humanoids in any meaningful way. I am not exaggerating here.

Now that you've realized that stuff can be pretty serious, you'll be relieved to know that I have lots of advice about it—advice that is based on all of the true stories that women have told me about stuff.

Take it from me: This is good stuff.

▲▲▲▲▲▲▲▲▲▲▲▲▲▲▲▲▲▲▲▲▲▲▲▲

His Stuff That's Still at Your House

After the split, you're bound to find something of your ex's lying around, even if you scoured your house from top to bottom the day of the breakup in an admirable attempt to rid yourself of all reminders of the scumbag. It's an unpleasant post-breakup truth that at least one object your ex leaves behind will somehow find its way to a remote cubbyhole, where it will lie in wait until it can jump out at you when you least expect it. You will be innocently looking under the kitchen sink for a replacement lightbulb when suddenly one of your ex's golf tees will slide out from under the dust bunny it was using as camouflage and roll into your line of vision, whereupon you will shriek "*Aieee!*" and run around your house as if you'd just been attacked by a swarm of killer bees.

This is all due to the

"My fiancé broke up with me right before the wedding. We caused a huge scene in Williams-Sonoma. He wanted credit on all of the gifts his family had bought; I said no way."
—Trish, Austin

Law of Motion and Emotion, which—as those of you who took physics will remember—states:

> A body remains in constant motion with a constant velocity unless you throw it at your ex and it gets lodged under the sofa, whereupon you will forget about it until months after the breakup, when, exerting much force, you will move said couch and uncover said body, whereupon you will begin to run around your apartment at an accelerated velocity while waving your arms in equal but opposite directions, prompting your neighbors to call 911.

You probably think that coming across your ex's golf tee (or any other object he once owned or touched) wouldn't bother *you*, right? You wouldn't put it in your scrapbook, or under your pillow, or in your shadowbox, right? You'd just throw it away, right? *Right?!?*

If you immediately answered "Right!," congratulations: You are a Big Fat Liar. Don't try to deny it. Remember: *It's the nineties, and in the nineties, we relate to material things much better than we relate to people.* Consider these scary true stories:

▲ One woman purposely keeps a few pieces of her ex's clothing, so she can "smell them." (I presume she's not talking about underwear here.)

▲ After a big breakup, another woman walked around her apartment for two whole days *clutching to her chest the plate her ex had given her.* "It was an artistic Chinese plate" was this woman's lame excuse.

▲ One woman's ex left numerous things behind—furniture, records, his prized Minnesota Twins signed baseball—and *used them as an excuse to call or drop by every few weeks*. "We broke up almost two years ago, and he's *still* calling me about the damn baseball," she says.

▲ One woman kept her ex's condiments. "We broke up seven years ago, and I still have his Worcestershire sauce. It brings back great memories."

▲ Another woman kept her boyfriend's feather pillow out of "pure spite" because it had belonged to his grandmother.

▲ And one woman said that, after the breakup, "My ex made a list of all the things he'd left at my house. My sister and I couldn't *believe* it. He remembered everything—even his replacement razors. If he'd clipped his nose hairs in my apartment the day before, he would have wanted the nose hairs. It wasn't about the stuff; he was just being horrible. So I kept a few of his things just to piss him off."

As you can see from these examples, post-breakup stuff can serve two important functions:

1. You can use it to control your ex's emotions and behavior in some really fun ways.
2. You can cling to it obsessively and pretend that as long as you have it, you and your ex will be linked romantically.

The only problem with these tactics (aside from the fact that they're highly unhealthy) is that, in many cases, *your ex will be able to use them, too*. Which leads us to . . .

▲▲▲▲▲▲▲▲▲▲▲▲▲▲▲▲▲▲▲▲▲▲▲▲▲▲▲

Your Stuff That's Still at His House

If you've left anything at your ex's house, you will suddenly find that the controlling shoe is on the other foot. Many unpleasant scenarios may ensue.

▲ If he did the breaking up, you will call him three times a day, ostensibly to ask for your stuff back, but *really* to ask for your ex back. "Hi, it's me," you'll say. "Listen, I think you have my sweater. Can I have it back?" And your ex will reply, "Sure." You will take this positive response as a sign that he still cares about you, and you will suddenly burst out, *"I don't really want the sweater! I want you!"* And you will start crying, which will cause your ex to feel so guilty that he'll keep the sweater instead of giving it to his sister, which will give *you* another opportunity to call about getting the sweater back, etc. This will go on for maybe five years.

▲ If you did the breaking up and your ex is still crazy about you, he will call you three times a day and say things like, "I have your sweater. In fact, I'm touching it right now. Ooh, it feels so soft. I can't help thinking about how great you looked in it. Ooh . . ." And you will be forced to slam down the receiver in disgust.

▲ If you did the breaking up and he now hates your guts, he will use your stuff as an excuse to call three times a day and taunt you. For example, I once made the mistake of storing my air conditioner at my boyfriend's place for the winter. When I broke up with him the following spring, I forgot all about it. So there I was, feeling strong, feeling like I'd made the right decision, when suddenly the phone rings and my ex says, "Hey, just wanted you to know I've still got your air conditioner and you're not getting it back! Nyah nyah nyah-nyah nyah!" And I immediately felt like *crap*. "Stupid idiot!" I said to myself, smacking myself on the forehead. "Why couldn't you have broken up with him *after* you got your air conditioner back?!"

Note: It didn't take me very long to get over this particular ex, but it took me a helluva long time to get over the loss of my air conditioner. Especially since the following summer was the hottest in New York City history.

And don't think that you'll only be obsessed with the *expensive* things you left at your ex's. You'll be obsessed with the trivial things, too. I once got all bent out of shape because one of my exes kept the brand-new $7 bottle of aloe vera gel I'd lent him, even after I asked for it back.

If the gel had dropped out of my purse and rolled into the sewer I wouldn't have given a damn, but because my ex had it, I wanted it like I'd never wanted anything before. I developed an extremely irrational attachment to it. I became consumed with desire for it. It was my most prized possession *and my ex had it*.

It's pretty obvious that it wasn't really the aloe vera that was bothering me. It was the fact that my ex had caused me pain and turmoil *and* I was out $7. This final insult was just too much. I'm embarrassed to admit that, at the height of my aloe-induced hysteria, I even considered taking my ex to *small claims court*. Fortunately, the effects of the tequila wore off before I could go through with this plan, and I realized that (1) it was ridiculous, (2) it would require me to see my ex's stupid face, and (3) it was therefore not worth the trouble.

Plus, I didn't have a receipt for the aloe, so I couldn't prove beyond a reasonable doubt that it was really mine.

▲▲▲▲▲▲▲▲▲▲▲▲▲▲▲▲▲▲▲▲▲▲▲▲▲

The Big Switch

If you're a sane person and feel okay about returning all of your ex's stuff to him, and you're lucky enough to have an ex who feels the same, you will need to schedule an MTRS, or Meeting to Return Stuff. This will consist of your putting your ex's stuff in a box and meeting him at a predetermined time at some designated neutral spot, where he'll be with a box of *your* stuff. If all goes well, you'll make a quick and painless switch, and then you'll both ride into your respective sunsets.

The only problem with the MTRS is that, no matter how amicably you and your ex parted, it never goes well. Sometimes he (or you) forgets to put something *really important* in said box, whereupon he (or you) is called a "big thief." Sometimes you can't decide on a neutral spot, so you end up meeting at an extremely un-neutral spot, such as the romantic restaurant where you first had sex. Sometimes the sight of you will prompt him to ask, "Have you slept with anyone since me?" and (if you've been paying attention to

my advice at all) you will reply in the affirmative, whereupon an ugly scene will ensue.

But the most common scenario is the one wherein you
schedule the MTRS, arrive at the designated spot at the
designated time, and wait for your ex to show. Hours pass.
Soon you begin to think you got the time wrong, or the day,
or the place. You become concerned that your ex will think
you did this on purpose, and you are so eager to prove that
you're Bigger Than That that you schlepp his stuff *back*
to your house and call him on the phone. Whereupon you
find out that he left two days ago for the Bahamas and never
intended to meet with you in the first place.

If your ex is stringing you along with the MTRS thing, then
let your stuff go and just return his stuff to him. It remains
one of life's biggest ironies that *the best way to control someone who wants to control you is to let go of whatever it is they're
trying to control you with.*

Of course, it's possible that you have a very wily ex, one
who knows that if you're big enough to let him keep *your*
stuff, then you're going to be really upset if you can't return
his stuff. The wily ex knows that the stuff he left at your
house will soon become like Poe's tell-tale heart: It will take
on a life of its own. You will feel a stab of guilt every time
you look at it, because it's visual proof that you have not
done the right thing. Soon the stuff will begin to pulsate
and throb with the most horrifying sound—lubDUB—
without stopping—lubDUB—day and night—lubDUB.
Eventually, this sound will drive you insane.

You could prevent all of this, of course, by simply throwing his stuff away, but that will make you feel even *more* guilty, because in this day of Reduce, Reuse, Recycle, throwing away perfectly good stuff is a virtual *blasphemy*.

Instead, try these tactics, which were recommended to me by various women who used them:

▲ Inform your ex that if he doesn't come and collect his stuff ASAP, it will be put out in the driveway for him— or various passersby—to pick up at will.
▲ UPS it to his office.
▲ Give it away. One woman gave her ex's Armani tie to her brother for Christmas. Another kept her ex's boxer shorts and then gave them to her next boyfriend. "It was my way of saying, 'Ha! I've found someone who can fill your shorts!'" she says.

Sometimes, however, there are extenuating circumstances that prevent you from getting rid of your ex's stuff. This seems as good a place as any to share with you the best (or worst, depending on how you look at it) story about post-breakup stuff that I've ever heard. It came from a woman who initially professed not to *have* any post-breakup stuff. Naturally, I was skeptical. The ensuing conversation went something like this:

ME: You are *sure* you have absolutely nothing around the house that reminds you of your ex? Nothing he gave you?
HER: He didn't ever give me anything.
ME: No cards? No letters? No pictures?
HER: No. Well . . . there is one thing, but I'm not sure it counts as "stuff" the way you mean it.

ME: Aha! I knew it! What is it?

HER: Well . . . I have my ex.

ME: What?

HER: His ashes.

ME: *What?*

HER: In an urn. On my mantel.

ME: *What?!*

Turns out that she once dated a guy for two weeks. A few months after she broke up with him, he died in a motorcycle accident. She had to handle all of the funeral arrangements, since his brother—his only living relative—lived thousands of miles away and couldn't deal. So she had her ex cremated, as he'd wished, and then she called his brother to find out when he was coming to get the ashes.

"I can't right now, because I'm in the process of moving," he told her. "Can you hold on to them for a while? I'll call you as soon as I've settled in."

"That was two years ago," she says. "I still have the ashes, because I don't know what to do with them. It's really getting me down. I haven't dated anyone since this happened, and sometimes I think that the spirit of my ex is preventing me from getting dates."

I was momentarily stunned by the macabre vision of an ex reaching out from beyond the grave to scare away potential suitors. Fortunately, I recovered just in time to tell her what to do, which was to run, not walk, to her ex's favorite place—be it the ocean, the local nudie bar, or the bathroom toilet—and immediately dispose of the ashes.

"Don't sprinkle them, *dump* them," I said. "Then get the hell out of there." I don't know whether she took the advice or not.

It would take a very sick person to find anything funny about this story, so let me assure you that I am that person. Anyway, I got to thinking that this story would make a great horror movie: Woman dates man. Man dies. Woman keeps ashes in urn on mantel. Woman dates another man. Kisses him in front of urn. Urn begins to vibrate and then flies across room, hitting new beau in head and killing him. Another urn appears on mantel. And so on, until woman finally dates an exorcist who frees the trapped spirits of all the exes. The movie ends with the ghosts of the exes high-fiving each other and then heading to the local playground, where they play an invisible game of pickup basketball.

As I ruminated on the finer points of the screenplay and mentally composed my Oscar acceptance speech, I suddenly remembered an article I'd clipped from the *Dallas Morning News*. The title of the article was "Can't Part with Fido? Freeze-Dry Him," and it was about a Colorado Springs company that freeze-dries dead animals into "lifelike" poses so that their owners can keep them for all eternity. Dead-pet owners were apparently champing at the bit, so to speak, to take advantage of this opportunity. I, of course, immediately wondered if it would work on people.

I made a quick call to the company (Timberline Taxidermy, in case you're interested) and was informed that, theoretically, it would. All they'd have to do is ice your ex's corpse until it reached 180 degrees below zero, and then put it into a vacuum chamber and suck all the moisture out of it.

The process *is* expensive—freeze-drying a 9-pound pet

costs $550, so freeze-drying a 200-pound ex would cost about $110,000—but think about the possibilities. You could have them pose your ex so it looks like he's begging for forgiveness. You could have them pose him in a sitting position, put him on your couch and tell your parents you're married. (They'll be none the wiser, especially if you insert a remote into his lifeless hands.) You could even have them pose your ex so he's standing up with his arms sticking straight out at the sides, and then you could use him as a coat rack.

But I digress. It's time to get back to the subject at hand, which is, if I remember correctly, "stuff."

▲▲▲▲▲▲▲▲▲▲▲▲▲▲▲▲▲▲▲▲▲▲▲▲▲▲

When Your POSSLQ (Person of Opposite Sex Sharing Living Quarters) Becomes Your POSLFFYHP (Person of Opposite Sex Living as Far from You as Humanly Possible)

The "stuff" question becomes much more complicated if you and your ex lived together, especially if you and he actually shared things.

COMPLICATION #1: You forget whose stuff is whose. When you've been using something every day for two years, you tend to think it's yours, even if someone else technically paid for it. This problem is often exacerbated on Post-Breakup Moving Day, because—and this is a well-known fact—psychological trauma causes temporary paralysis of the brain cells. On moving day, your brain cells might be so paralyzed that you and your ex won't even be able to make *educated guesses* as to who owns what.

"Is this your hip vinyl backpack with the big yellow sunflowers on it?" you'll ask your soon-to-be-ex.

"Yes," he'll say absentmindedly. "Is this your hockey puck?"

"Don't be an idiot," you'll reply. "Of *course* it's my hockey puck."

Later, you will both realize your mistake, and you'll have to have one of those dreaded MTRSs I've talked about.

COMPLICATION #2: You and your ex will have joint ownership of many expensive objects, and you'll both want them. There are many ways to handle this problem. One is to sit down with your ex, make a list of all joint purchases, and bargain, bargain, bargain. "My husband and I split everything down the middle when we got divorced," one woman told me. "I let him have the house, the microwave, the recliner, two lamps, and the kitchen table and chairs. It was only when I moved into my new apartment that I realized *I didn't have anywhere to sit down.* If it happened to me now, I'd take everything, *and* I'd get alimony."

Which leads us to the other, more mature option—namely, faking out your ex by letting him have everything, and then stealing it all back the next time he leaves town. This is a time-honored technique passed down to us from prehistoric times. We know this because, in 1902, Sir Edmund O'Leary found the words "Ung Ug, Urg Ah" written on the wall of a cave in southern France; this was later found to be the first known usage of the phrase "Finders keepers, losers weepers."

The problem with the old "losers weepers" technique is that it, too, can be used against you. Here's one woman's horror story:

"I lived with a guy for four years. I wasn't home when he moved out, so he took *everything*. He took the stereo and the TV. He took the plants. He took the garden hose, the egg timer, the tool box. He took the patio furniture. He even took the telephone. It was just like *How the Grinch Stole Christmas*. I went from having a furnished apartment with a king-sized bed and six pairs of sheets to having a plastic stool and a clock radio. I had to sleep on the floor."

But this woman had chutzpa. The day after her ex cleaned her out, she went to an electronics store, went up to the guy at the service desk, and said, "I need to buy a stereo, a TV, a VCR, a telephone, an answering machine, and a few other things." The guy got the manager.

"The trip to the electronics store was very cathartic," said the woman. "I ended up buying five speakers with surround sound that were so big I had to buy wall brackets. I bought a Yamaha 260-watt receiver. I bought a 27-inch Mitsubishi black-diamond screen TV with every feature in the world in it, and I had them throw in a black glass TV stand. I don't know how to program any of this stuff, but damn it, it's mine."

COMPLICATION #3: You and your ex have things in storage. This is a common problem in larger cities, where most apartments are the size of your average Roach Motel. The problem with having things in storage is that you usually forget they're there until well after you've split from your ex. One woman, for example, kept on paying for the storage because she thought it was mostly her stuff. Two years later she went to clean it out and discovered that everything in the space belonged to her ex and she'd basically thrown thousands of dollars out the window.

Another woman's husband offered to pay for the storage himself and then took a "To Hell with It" attitude. Result: The storage company auctioned off her collection of original jazz recordings from the forties, her antique Kodak camera, and, ironically, her wedding album. Worst of all, they auctioned off her *vintage Barbies*, which she'd had since childhood.

So I guess the best piece of advice I can offer about this storage issue is that you should live in a really, really big apartment, preferably alone.

▲▲▲▲▲▲▲▲▲▲▲▲▲▲▲▲▲▲▲▲▲▲▲▲

The Gifts

It's very important that you don't give back any of the gifts your ex bought you. Some women do, with the misguided notion that it makes them appear noble and dignified. To them I say: *puh-lease!* If you don't want the stuff, sell it and use the money to buy something that would really piss your ex off, such as condoms or a vibrator. (Men hate vibrators. They have Vibrator Envy. I know this because when my

> "I do regret giving my ex's Ray•Bans away. He'd given them to me on our first real date. We'd spent the day driving around, listening to great music and sharing stories about ourselves. It was sunny, so I grabbed his Ray•Bans off the dashboard and put them on. When I went to take them off at the end of the date, he said, 'Keep them. I like the idea of you having them.' It was such a perfect day."
> —Kyra, Louisville

friend Katie's husband found her vibrator, he got a hammer and broke it into a million pieces.)

And speaking of gifts: One woman's ex had the audacity to demand that she *give back* the cappuccino machine he'd bought her for Christmas. "He told me that he didn't want me to use it with someone else," she said. "God forbid I make a cup of cappuccino for another guy."

If *your* ex asks you to return a gift he bought you, simply call the Taste Police and have him arrested for being too tacky for words.

It's especially important that you keep any gifts your ex bought you that are actually useful. I, for example, held on to the following gifts purchased by various exes:

▲ My TV
▲ My toaster oven
▲ My videocassette player (as opposed to videocassette *recorder*, which my ex was too cheap to buy me)

▲ My huge beveled mirror, which my ex salvaged from a construction site
▲ My Ray•Ban sunglasses
▲ My London Fog raincoat
▲ My pearl necklace
▲ My Indian-patterned rug
▲ My Vivitar camera
▲ My sexy beaded top

Keep an open mind when assessing the utility of the stuff your ex gave you, because you may realize, with sudden and blinding insight, that something you originally thought was a worthless piece of crap actually serves a less obvious but highly important purpose. For example, when Jennifer Flavin was dumped by Sly Stallone, she discovered that the bronze casting of his arm made a mighty fine paperweight. You may find that the ugly plastic tray your ex bought you, the one that says "Missouri: the 'You Show Me Yours, I'll Show You Mine' State," makes a keen receptacle for Kitty Litter.

If you *really* don't want the stuff around, you have three options:

1. If the gift is an item of clothing, take it to Nordstrom's and return it for a full refund. I would love to tell you about how Nordstrom's is such a great store that they'll take things back without a receipt, *even* if the item was purchased in 1972 and you're not 100 percent sure it really came from Nordstrom's. But they'd probably sue me.
2. If the item definitely wasn't purchased at Nord-

strom's and therefore cannot be returned, take it to the mall, go to the top floor, and throw it over the railing. One woman told me that this worked for her.

3. If the item is a piece of jewelry, get it melted down and made into a new piece. Some jewelers who provide this service will even let *you* wield the blowtorch, the idea being that it's extremely cathartic to see the piece of metal that once symbolized your future melt slowly into a shapeless blob.

Warning: When you take your jewelry in to get it melted down, you may find out that the "diamond" your ex bought you is really a cubic zirconia that came out of a bubble gum machine. If this happens, you have my permission to send it back to your ex with the message, "Thanks for nothing, you cheap bastard."

▲▲▲▲▲▲▲▲▲▲▲▲▲▲▲▲▲▲▲▲▲▲▲▲

The Paper Trail of Love

Paper stuff is the toughest to deal with, because it tends to involve *good* memories of your ex and therefore has the power to actually make you miss the spitwad.

There's a right way and a wrong way to deal with paper stuff.

Wrong: Surround yourself with all of your photo albums and scrapbooks and torture yourself by looking at pictures of you and your ex in happier times, reading the love letters and cards he sent you, etc., until you become so maudlin that none of your friends want to hang out with you anymore.

Right: Surround yourself with all of your photo albums and scrapbooks and start throwing some of the stuff away. You can accomplish this odious task in eight easy steps:

Step 1: Separate all of your relationship mementos into three piles. In the first pile (hereafter known as the Good Pile), put everything that feeds your ego. In the second pile (hereafter known as the Bad Pile), put everything that makes you want to gag, cry, or kill. In the third pile (hereafter known as the Pile with No Name), put all of your journals, plus any love letters your ex(es) may have sent you.

Step 2: Get rid of the Bad Pile. You can maximize the therapeutic benefits by choosing one of the following techniques:

▲ Burn it.
▲ Tear it all up and toss it, confetti-like, into your toilet. (Putting your ex where he belongs, metaphorically speaking, is *very* satisfying, but be careful not to flush too much at once. One woman who tried this technique told me that her toilet got stopped up three times.)
▲ Take the scissors to it. This technique works best on photos in which your ex is alone or *you really look like crap*. (If it's a good picture of you, put it in the Good Pile. I'll tell you how to deal with it later.)

For a really fun time, cut out your ex's eyes, mouth, and you-know-what, and then put all of the random pieces in a Baggie and mail it to him. This will really creep him out.

Warning: Under no circumstances should you cut your ex out of the picture and keep the rest, because this will only remind you of the big hole he's left in your life.

Step 3: On to the Pile with No Name. First, take all of the sappy love letters he wrote you and put them in a box by themselves. Hide the box at the very top of your closet, way back behind your black-light posters and your Etch-A-Sketch, and forget about it until that point in time when you or your future children can pull it out, read the letters, and giggle hysterically.

Why keep these?

▲ Your ex will be sweating over them for the rest of his life, knowing that you and your children are giggling hysterically.
▲ If he ever becomes famous, you can make lots of money by selling the movie rights.
▲ They are concrete proof that a man once found you desirable.

Step 4: Go through your journals and underline the passages where, during the relationship, you complained about your ex, called him a jerk, etc. This will keep you from putting rose-colored glasses on the relationship and thinking that your ex was actually okay and you were a fool to let him go.

I tried this technique myself and was surprised to find many, many negative passages about various exes—even those that I still kind of liked. These negative passages typically began with the sentence *"I hate this relationship!"* and ended with the sentence *"I hate this relationship!"* In between were some of the specific things that I hated, such as . . .

▲ How one ex constantly talked about past girlfriends
▲ How another ex was always blowing me off and never called when he said he would
▲ How another ex would say sexist things just to make me mad
▲ How another ex had to have the TV on at all times, even when he was sleeping
▲ How this same ex got out and literally kissed the ground after I took his new Jeep for a test drive, and
▲ How another ex was a selfish, lying, ignorant, inconsiderate, immature moron, and I hope he dies.

In summary, your journals will help you put your past relationships in perspective. They also serve as important reminders of the self you used to be. And if you read them objectively, they can make you aware of the self-destructive patterns that are preventing you from having a *good* relationship.

This said, I should probably warn you that reading all of your journals in one sitting is *not* a good idea. I actually learned this while researching this book. One day I was sitting at my computer brainstorming, and I thought, "Hey! Maybe if I go through all of my journals, I'll find some more things to write about!"

This idea turned out to be both brilliant and incredibly stupid. Brilliant because yes, I *did* find more things to write about. Incredibly stupid because I was hit with a barrage of bad memories—memories that, until this point, I'd done a pretty good job of repressing. Reading about all of my failed relationships in one fell swoop put me into a depression that lasted for two whole weeks.

Worse, it caused me to have *recurring nightmares* about ex-boyfriends I hadn't thought about in years.

RECURRING NIGHTMARE #1: The setting: a basketball court. The hoop is about 50 feet away and about 30 feet high. There are two tall poles right in front of the hoop, set exactly the ball's width apart. Two men in suits are standing courtside. I'm supposed to make a basket, but it's nearly impossible—especially because I can't even hold on to the ball. I'm running all around the court, trying to catch it, when in walks my jock ex-boyfriend. He proceeds to swish shot after shot.

RECURRING NIGHT-MARE #2: An ex who dumped me has decided to give me a second chance. He's parked outside my apartment in a white convertible, waiting impatiently with the engine running. I'm frantically trying to pack two big suitcases, but as soon as I think I have everything, I turn around and there's another big pile of stuff to pack. I keep run-

> "My ex and I got back together, but it only lasted a few months. He made me a nice dinner—the only time he'd ever cooked for me—and I had diarrhea for *ten days*. I thought, 'God is trying to tell me something here.'"
> —Leila, Jersey City

ning to the door to make sure my ex is still there. In the end, he drives off without me.

RECURRING NIGHTMARE #3: I am in an apartment that has two doors that don't lock. A strange man is trying to get me. I'm terrified. I have one rubber doorstop, and I run from door to door, putting the doorstop under the door at the exact second that the strange man tries to open it. This goes on for some time. At last I miss, and the strange man gets into the apartment. Suddenly I see one of my exes standing outside the door. "Help me!" I plead. My ex gives me a blank look and just stands there as the strange man stabs me in the stomach with a butcher knife.

So as I was saying, it's not a good idea to read all of your journals in one sitting.

Step 5: It's now time to put your journals away and turn to the Good Pile. Begin by collecting all of those pictures of you and your ex in which you look incredibly fabulous. Instead of cutting your ex out and leaving half a picture (or, worse, a picture with a big hole in it), you are going to *take him out of the picture while leaving said picture completely intact*. There are a couple of ways you can work this magic. The cheapest and easiest involves going through an issue of *People* magazine, cutting out the head of a good-looking actor, and gluing it over your ex's face. The more expensive and more convincing way involves using a photo-retouching service. These services, using state-of-the-art techniques, can either

▲ "Erase" your ex from the picture, making it look like you were just standing there alone with your arm around thin air, or

▲ Flawlessly replace your ex with a picture of someone else, so it looks like you really *did* marry Brad Pitt.

Is technology great, or what?

Step 6: Take what's left of the Good Pile (all the cards, dried flowers, ticket stubs, pictures you didn't want to retouch, etc.), put it into a box, and have a friend or family member hold it for you for six months or so. *This step is very important, because it protects you from yourself.* If you get The Box out of your house, you won't be tempted to go through it every time you miss your ex—and this will greatly reduce your post-breakup misery.

Step 7: When the six months are up, get The Box back and open it. One of two things will happen:

▲ A really scary demon like the ones in *Raiders of the Lost Ark* will fly out and turn you into dust.

▲ You will find that you can look at the stuff *without getting really upset*. This momentous discovery will make you fall to the floor in a dead faint.

Here are three good reasons to open The Box after six months.

1. It will become a physical testament to your progress. Getting over an ex happens very gradually in tiny, tiny in-

crements, so you might not have realized how far you've come.

2. The passage of time will enable you to look at the contents objectively. This will give you new insights into your ex and your relationship. Here's what some women said:

▲ "My ex once sent me flowers with a card that said, 'Light. Heat. Your eyes.' At the time, I thought that was the most romantic thing ever. But when I looked at the card six months later, I realized he'd simply plagiarized a Peter Gabriel song."

▲ "My ex hated having his picture taken, even though he was an actor. When I opened my scrapbook a year later and saw all of the pictures of him covering his face, I finally realized that, yes, this guy was a *weirdo*."

▲ "I have a photo-booth picture of my ex and me French-kissing. When we first broke up, I couldn't even *look* at it, because I missed him so much. Now I look at it and think, 'Wow, Mom was right! He *is* kind of ugly.'"

3. You will find that some of the stuff is no longer meaningful. Trust me: There will be things in The Box that will prompt you to say, "What the *hell* is this, and why did I keep it?" Tossing these things will enable you to weed down the contents of The Box until only the important things are left.

Step 8: For best results, put The Box away and don't open it for another six months. Then repeat the weeding process. Eventually, you'll have the contents pared down to just those things that bring back really good memories. From that point on, looking through The Box will give you a pleasant feeling of nostalgia instead of an unpleasant feeling of intense agony. Which is as it should be.

Steps 7 and 8 are the most important parts of the Paper Stuff Removal Process. *If you do not follow steps 7 and 8, that Stephen King thing will start to happen and The Box will become so scary that you'll be afraid to open your closet door.* This is what happened to my sister, Tammy.

Over the years, she had crammed a shoe box with relationship mementos until it became *two* boxes—and then she never opened the boxes again.

Since many women I talked to were in similar situations, I thought it would be really helpful to have my sister sit down, go through her boxes, and give a blow-by-blow account of the experience. My thinking here was, "If she does this and then goes wacko, I probably won't recommend this tactic to my readers."

So I asked Tammy to open her boxes and analyze the contents for me.

"Okay," she reluctantly agreed, much doubt in her voice. "But I'll have to prepare myself. And I'll have to have a few beers first."

"It's not the Irish decathlon," I replied. "But do whatever you have to do." We agreed that I'd call her back later.

Note: The following is a transcript of what my sister said during the long and incredibly costly phone conversation that accompanied The Opening of The Boxes. *What you are* *about to read is true. The names have been changed to protect the indigent.**

Okay, so I have two shoe boxes here, both filled with guy-related stuff. I'm opening the first box now. *(Pauses to take a swig of beer.)* The stuff on top is all from my relationship with Gary, who moved to Chicago while we were dating. Bummer—I was really crazy about him. Okay, we have here a postcard from Wulff's Island Motel in Wisconsin. Here's a business card from Poet's, a bar in Chicago. Here's a Sweet'n Low packet from TGIFriday's, and a napkin from a bar called Mother's. Oh, here's a movie ticket—*Hamburger Hill*. Here are some chopsticks—they don't bring back a specific memory, so I'll send them to you. Here's a ticket to a football game. I sat in row 21, seat 25. Hmm, what's this? Oh, it's a list of all the times I visited Gary. I drove to Chicago every other weekend for two years. I'll keep it—it proves he liked me.

Here are two New Year's Eve blowers. *(Sound of horn.)* This one still works. *(Sound of someone spitting in my ear.)* This one doesn't. Throw it away. Here's the last of the Gary things—it's a chocolate heart. It brings back good memories, but I don't remember of what. Guess I should toss it, huh?

(Takes a long swig of beer.) Here's a flower card. Should I keep it if it doesn't mean anything to me

---

*This is an inside joke. Many of my sister's exes didn't even have a penny for their thoughts. (Not that their thoughts were worth a penny.)

and I didn't like the guy? No, you're right. That wouldn't be exorcising.

Okay. This stuff is all from my boyfriend Roy. Here's a map from Worlds of Fun. He made me go on all the rides, even though they made me sick. Throw it away. Here's an "I'm Sorry" card that says, "Sometimes I say or do things that I don't really mean. This is one of those times. I'm sorry." I'll keep it because it means I was right. Oh! Here's a note that says, "Tammy: You are the *best*, most beautiful, caring, lovable, sexy, delicious woman I've ever known. I will always suffer for what I've done and haven't done." He felt so bad. I'll keep it.

Oh, here's the card from the flowers that Danny sent me after he cheated on me. "How about another chance?" Yeah, right. Well, I'll keep it—it reminds me how guilty he felt. Oh, this is good. It's from when I dated that drummer. It's a copy of his band's touring schedule. And here's a backstage pass. I got in free and was escorted through the crowd. Isn't that cool? I'll keep it.

Okay, I'm at the bottom of the first box. What's this? It's a red felt heart that says "Guess Who?" Sorry, don't remember. Going in the trash.

I am now opening the second box. This is all stuff from Don. He was really into writing me notes and poems; he'd leave them on my car under the windshield wiper. Here's one on yellow stationery. Oh, he wrote this one after I broke up with him. It says, "I don't want to lose you but if I have already done that, will you still be my friend. Because you've always been my *best friend!!*" "Best friend" is under-lined twice.

Here's another juicy one. I think he was drunk when he wrote this one; the handwriting's different. And there's no punctuation, by the way. It says, "I still want you and I still love you very much I can't think of being without you please talk to me love don PS I just drove by to put this on your car." *(We laugh uproariously.)* That's a keeper—it's funny.

Oh! Here's another drunken letter with no punctuation. *(Takes another swig of beer.)* He spelled my name with only one "m." He always did that—it really pissed me off. Anyway, it says, "Tamy I wrote this poem for you the other night at work you probe think its corny but its how I feel." Oh—this is a crack up. I'll read it to you exactly the way he wrote it, with the misspellings and everything.

Every time that I close my eyes alls I see are
    those big brown eyes
I long to hold you in my Arms
Agian I wish it hadn't been the way its been
I miss you smell, I miss your smile
I miss your Strubnen* ways
Alls I can say for my sleff is I sorry
and I hope you'll be mine
agian someday.

(We laugh for a good fifteen minutes.)

*We think he meant stubborn, but we're not sure.

Well, the poem was the last item in the second box, which meant that the experiment was over. My sister and I agreed that it was a resounding success: Tammy's trash can was half full, and she said she felt like a huge weight had been lifted off her shoulders.

"I was so afraid to look in those boxes," she said. "I thought I was going to get really upset. But a lot of the things didn't bother me at all, which is kind of surprising because they were all very important to me at one time. I feel like I'm really *over* these guys."

It is our hope that the advice in this chapter will have the same effect on you.

10

Can You—Should You—Stay Friends with Your Ex?

SURE, if you live on the planet Zorgon, where men and women coexist in complete harmony. Here on Earth, however, it's not a good idea.

Allow me to explain. The fact that it's virtually impossible to be friends with an ex has absolutely *nothing* to do with the old *When Harry Met Sally* line, "Men and women can't be friends." No, it's just that once you've

> "The hardest thing about breaking up—no matter who does it—is that you're losing the person you confide in most. You want to call him and say, 'Help, I'm really hurting,' but you can't, because he's the *reason* you hurt."
> —Jenny, Cedar Rapids

played Hide the Salami with a guy (or Hide the Gherkin, as the case may be), it's very hard to go back to a platonic relationship.

The major problem is that one of you almost always has an ulterior motive (i.e., sex). The person who has this ulterior motive is usually the person who didn't want to break up in the first place. This person will do anything to keep the other person in his or her life, and if being friends is the only way to do that, then friends they will be. Sure, we're just friends now, but soon we'll be sleeping together again, is what they're thinking.

The other person in this equation tends to fall into one of five categories:

The Saint. *Motto:* "I would rather sleep with a gorilla than with my ex, but it would be mean to say so." *Characteristics:* ▲ Needs to be liked. ▲ Hates hurting people's feelings. ▲ Master of the Little White Lie. *Reasoning:* "By remaining friends with my ex, I'm letting him down easy." *Doesn't realize that:* Being kind to an ex because you feel sorry for him is dishonest and will only give him false hope. *Real-life result:* May make your ex hate you even more. "My ex said he really cared about me and still wanted me in his life—just not 'that way.' He thought he was doing me a favor, when really he was just filling me with doubt and confusion. I'll never forgive him for that."

The Wimp. *Motto:* "I'd like to break it off entirely, but there'd probably be an ugly scene." *Characteristics:* ▲ Hates conflict. ▲ Indecisive. ▲ Weak-willed. *Reasoning:* "If I put up with the friend thing long enough, my ex will break it off himself." *Doesn't realize that:* Your ex will sense your weakness and interpret it as a sign that you still care, whereupon he will redouble his efforts to get you back into bed. *Real-life result:* A really, really ugly scene. "My ex fiancé was kind of a wacko, but I still talked to him whenever he called because I couldn't deal with moving or changing my phone number. Eventually he started coming to my house and begging me for sex, and I finally had to call the police."

The Emotional Cripple. *Motto:* "My ex knows me so well. If I break it off with him completely, who will I go to when I have a problem?" *Characteristics:* ▲ Dependent on others. ▲ Afraid of being alone. ▲ Afraid of change. *Doesn't realize that:* Self-reliance is the key to self-esteem. Using your ex as a crutch until you meet your next lover prevents you from growing as a person. *Real-life result:* You may become increasingly self-centered and shallow. "There's a certain convenience in staying with a known quantity. Why end it completely? After all, you don't quit a job without having another job."

The Martyr. *Motto:* "I initiated the split, so I must pay the price." *Characteristics:* ▲ Plagued with guilt. ▲ Occasional feelings of self-hatred. ▲ Glutton for punishment. *Doesn't realize that:* Breaking up with someone doesn't make you a horrible person. *Real-life result:* Loss of self-respect. "My ex was so sweet when he wasn't being a complete jerk, so I just couldn't bring myself to break it off entirely. For three months, I let him take me out to dinner, buy me things, and basically drive me up the wall. It was sickening—it was like

I'd say 'Jump' and he'd say 'How high?' I'm so mad at myself for letting it continue."

The Egotist. *Motto:* "The more guys who call me, the better—even if they *are* ex-boyfriends." *Characteristics:* ▲ Superficial. ▲ Flirtatious. ▲ Self-esteem is based entirely on sexual attractiveness. *Doesn't realize that:* This is a form of greed—and greed in any form is very, very ugly. *Real-life result:* May end up with no one at all. "My roommate liked to keep all of her exes on a string. Whenever they'd call, she'd tease them by saying things like, 'I'm wearing that sweater you used to like so much.' Eventually, word got around, and now *no one* calls her—including the guy she really *does* like."

I think it's pretty safe to say that no matter which category you're in (or which side you're on), the post-breakup friend thing *really sucks*. Sooner or later, one of you is going to start feeling trapped, and the other, more desperate. Neither of you will be able to move forward. "I wasted a lot of energy on a relationship that my partner had decided was over long ago," one woman told me. "If he had just ended it instead of simply postponing the inevitable, I'd probably be over him by now."

Said another: "I agreed to stay friends with my ex, and it prevented me from meeting someone new. I just couldn't forgive myself for letting him stay in my life. Why didn't I have the guts to say no?"

The harsh truth is that most couples aren't friends to begin with—and if you aren't friends with your ex *before* the split, there's really no way in hell you're going to be friends *after* the split.

Also, relationships have a way of bringing out the worst in people, so even if you and your ex *were* friends at one time, that doesn't mean you're friends now.

You can test your post-breakup friendship potential by answering a few easy questions:

▲ When you and your ex discuss your feelings for each other, do you hold anything back?

▲ Will you tell your ex goodbye when you—or he—meets someone new?

▲ When your ex calls, do you feel a slight twinge of dread?

▲ When you're together, do you bicker constantly?

▲ Do you feel any sexual vibes for your ex—or vice versa?

If the answer to any of these questions is yes, then I have an important news bulletin for you: *The friendship thing is probably not going to work out.*

If, however, the answer to all of these questions is a resounding "No!," then by all means continue to attempt the friend thing. But first you might want to heed the following advice: "I've found that it's pretty hard to get over someone when you're seeing and talking to them regularly," said one woman. "It's better to take a few months off. That way, you both have time to change so that you no longer know each other quite so intimately. *Then* you can be friends."

You should know, however, that even if you do everything right, the friendship thing probably won't last: Future partners tend to feel threatened by lingering exes. "My ex and I cared deeply about each other, but his new girlfriend

hated me," said one woman. "She finally gave him an ulti-
matum: 'It's her or me.' He picked her."

"My ex and I now have a brother-sister relationship,"
said another. "Even so, my new boyfriend feels incredibly
jealous. He knows that I can talk to my ex about anything—and vice versa—and that makes him feel very left
out."

In most cases, it's best to junk the friend idea and make it a
clean break. Done. Finished. Over. Sure, your ex may hate
you for a while, but he'll get over it. And even if he doesn't,
chances are that *you will*.

11

What to Do When Your Ex Comes Crawling Back

OKAY, so you've said no to the friend thing, you've made a clean break, and you're realizing that Life Without Ex isn't so horrible. Murphy's Law says that as soon as you've reached this point of emotional strength, your ex will call you up and say something like, "I love you, and I need you, and you were the most wonderful thing in the whole world!"*

When it comes to exes, one thing's for damn sure: They have impeccable timing. There must be some strange, unerring masculine instinct that tells them when to call for maximum impact. If it takes you a year to get over them, they will call *one day* before that year is up. If it takes you three months to get over them, they'll call in three months.

"Over a five-year period, my ex would come back into my life just as I was getting over him," said one woman. "A

---

*This is an actual quote. Pathetic, isn't it?

few months would go by and I'd think, 'It's really over'—
and that *day* he'd call or come knocking at my door, or I'd
get a postcard in the mail. Each time I'd be hopeful for a few
weeks, then the grieving process would start all over again.
It was a vicious circle."

Another woman said it took her five years to get over
her ex, and just when she thought he was out of her system
for good, *he started calling her surreptitiously from his new girlfriend's house.* Here are some other women's experiences
with this bizarre phenomenon:

▲ "My fiancé walked out on me right before our wedding,
without giving me a reason. A year and a half later, I
went to Hawaii on a solo vacation and finally started
feeling that I was over him and that a new phase of my
life was beginning. Within a *week* of my return, he suddenly started sending me books, cards, love letters, and
dozens and dozens of roses."

▲ "I have this thing with guys that they never like me
until they've broken up with me. Six months later, they
come back to me, whining, 'You were the best thing that
ever happened to me! Why did I break up with you?'
'Because I made you feel good about yourself because I'm
an *idiot*,' is the answer."

▲ "A few months after my ex and I split up, someone
started making hang-up calls to me every fifteen minutes, at all hours. I knew it was my ex, so every few days
I'd call and tell him to cut it out. He would deny that it
was him and then try to draw me into conversation.
This went on for more than a year. Finally I got an un-
listed phone number."

The number-one question on these women's lips was: "*Why? Why* didn't he call me sooner, when I really missed him? Why did he wait until I was just starting to feel confident without him?"

There are a few possible explanations. One is scientific: Apparently there's a temporary post-breakup psychosis peculiar to men in which, long after the split, they suddenly think they're still in the relationship. They begin to talk about you in the first person, call you as if no time has passed, and send you creepy letters that say things like, "What's up with you? Why haven't you been talking to me this week?"

The legendary Thomas Disch* once said, "Creativity is the ability to see relationships where none exist," and maybe this is what he was talking about. However, don't let this highbrow observance stop you from dashing off a letter to your ex that says, "I haven't been talking to you because we broke up *two years ago*, stupid." *That* should burst his bubble.

Another explanation for the time-lag thing comes from one of the world's greatest thinkers, the wise philosopher and sagacious savant otherwise known as Madonna. "Rejection is the greatest aphrodisiac," she says in her song "Forbidden Love."

Hail to the all-knowing, all-seeing goddess of relationship wisdom. Oh wait—that's *me*. Well, hail to Madonna, too.

*No, I don't know who the hell he is, either.

The fact of the matter is, when a man breaks up with a woman, he doesn't fully think it through. He doesn't realize it means that he won't ever see her or speak to her again. This is due partly to egotism ("She'll never be able to live without me") and partly to stupidity ("She'll never be able to live without me"). Many men think they'll be able to call their ex-girlfriend whenever they want, and she'll immediately come running back. (This proves just how clueless men really are, poor things.)

When a guy realizes that a woman is *not* going to grovel and beg for his love, and, indeed, that she's virtually forgotten what he looks like, he takes this as a personal rejection of his manhood and decides that he must win her back at all costs.

Basically, it all boils down to the Challenge Factor. Relationships involve many, many cruel ironies, and this is one of the cruelest: The minute we pitiful human beings can't have something, *we want it like never before*. (It's kind of like that embarrassing aloe vera incident I told you about.)

In just seconds you go from being your ex's Personal Doormat to being his Holy Grail. So be prepared! He's going to pull out all the stops.

First, your ex will most probably attempt to disarm you by using the Creep Defense: "I was such a horrible boyfriend, I treated you like crap, I didn't deserve you, yadda yadda yadda." Blaming himself for the split serves three purposes: (1) It sounds like an apology, (2) it feeds your ego, and (3) it keeps you from hanging up.

Once he has your attention, he'll say he's changed. "I'm not that person anymore, I'm a new man, yadda yadda yadda." Then he will immediately appeal to your sense of compassion by making you feel sorry for him. "Since we split up, my life has been hell. I lost my job, my dog died, yadda yadda yadda."

Then he'll go for the K.O.: "I have to see you. If I don't see you, I might do something drastic, yadda yadda yadda."

Stand firm! Avoid seeing him at all costs! Before you let yourself be tempted by your ex's clever ploys, read these horror stories:

▲ "Two months after we broke up, my ex sent me a letter saying he'd 'really changed' and he'd 'always love me.' He'd never said he loved me before, so needless to say I was thrown for a loop. I foolishly agreed to a date. As soon as I saw him, I regretted it. He'd changed all right: He'd become even *more* annoying."

▲ "A year after the breakup, my ex invited me over to 'work in his garden.' Within minutes of my arrival, he'd hit on all my sore spots and had me in tears. Then he said, 'Don't cry. Let's go out to the garden,' and he gave me a little ax and a trowel. From that point on, I didn't hear a word he said. I just kept looking from the ax to him and thinking, 'Gee, I wonder what he'd look like with his head off.'"

▲ "My problem was worse. As soon as *I* saw my ex, I wanted him back. And the minute he knew he had me, he dumped me again."

Don't panic! There are many down-and-dirty tactics you can employ to get your ex out of your life once and for all.

Plan A: Nip it in the bud when he calls by either (1) pretending you're in the middle of sex, (2) adopting a foreign accent, or (3) making shrill beeping noises and saying, "The number you have dialed has been disconnected or is no longer in service."

Plan B: If these tactics don't work, get tough. "The next time your ex calls, say, 'I'm sorry, but from now on I'm going to hang up when I hear your voice,'" advised one woman. "And tell him that if he shows up at your door, you'll have no choice but to call the police. Then *go through with it*. If you don't, he won't take you seriously, and he'll see an open door."

Note: This tactic may take a while to work. One of my exes called me regularly after the breakup, even though I consistently hung up on him. I think the problem was my slow reaction time: He'd say, "Is Beth there?" and before I could stop myself, I'd automatically say, "Speaking." *Then* I'd realize who it was, and I'd immediately hang up. But it would be too late: I would have already said that one word. After about a year of this ("Is Beth there?" "Speaking." *Click*), he finally got the message. To keep this from happening to you, put my Fabulous Clip-n-Save Phone Call Response Chart by your telephone (see box, page 156).

Plan C: If your ex *still* won't take no for an answer, it's time to employ that most dreaded of tactics—namely, having another guy threaten him with bodily harm. "I broke up with my ex after he cheated on me," said one woman. "Two years later, he began calling repeatedly. Finally I said, 'Okay, why don't you come on over and we'll talk about us.' When he pulled into the driveway, I quickly called a beefy male friend and said, 'My ex-boyfriend is hounding me here and I'm really scared. Can you please come over?' Soon the doorbell rang and this huge guy came in, pointed at my ex, and said, 'If you don't leave *now*, I'm going to kick your ass!' It worked: My ex disappeared forever."

Note: Secondhand threats work, too. One woman told her ex: "My brothers said I should give you this message: If you ever bother me again, they're going to cut your $%*&# off." She hasn't heard from him since.

Plan D: If your ex is *still* in the picture, he probably senses that you're feeling conflicted, and that you are actually considering seeing him again.

I didn't want to have to do this, but you've given me no other choice: I am forced to reveal the Top-Secret, No-Holds-Barred 12-Step Program for Ex-Termination.

Note: The following information is For Your Eyes Only. Under no circumstances must anyone of the opposite sex* discover this secret, or *relationships as we know them will cease to exist.* For this reason, we members of the sisterhood ask that after reading the following passage, you *tear it out and eat it.* Thank you.

Step 1: Get your ex to come to your apartment. (*Do* not *meet on neutral ground.*)

Step 2: Arrange for a friend to call you while your ex is there.

*Code for "men."

Step 3: Before your ex arrives, cover your chairs, sofa, and bed with books, magazines, and piles of dirty clothes so there's only one place for him to sit. This "seat" must be something that's short, such as a stool or an ottoman.

Step 4: When your ex arrives, lead him into your apartment by putting your hand on the small of his back and giving a little pressure.

Step 5: Have him sit on the only seat available. Then take the books off of the highest chair you've got and pull it over so you're sitting directly in front of your ex, looking down at him.

Step 6: At this point your ex will start feeling a little nervous, and he may ask for a glass of water, an ashtray, etc. If he does, tell him to get it himself. *It is very important that you do not let your ex see the back of your head.*

Step 7: Using your best guidance counselor voice, ask your ex to tell you how he feels. Respond with "Hmms," "Uh-huhs," and sentences that begin, "It seems to me that . . ." *Don't* use the phrase "I feel," and don't place any blame.

Step 8: When your friend calls, as scheduled, pretend she's your new boyfriend. Giggle softly and say, "I can't talk right now." Then hang up.

Step 9: Bring the conversation with your ex to a close by saying, "I'm really sorry things are so messed up for you right now. Let me know if I can do anything to help." Act as if you really do feel sorry for him.

Step 10: Lead your ex to the door by once again putting your hand on the small of his back.

Step 11: Your ex will probably call in a few days. *Let the machine pick up, and do not return the call.*

Step 12: The next time you see your ex, muss up his hair and act like he's your little brother.

The woman who divulged this 12-step program to me *swore* that it's worked for everyone who's tried it. "It's a big power move, and it ensures that your ex's last view of you is one of dignity," she said. "After this he will *beg you* to come back, and you'll immediately lose all of your desire for him. Guaranteed."

Yes, the Challenge Factor strikes again. But this time, it's working in *your* favor.

Elizabeth Kuster's Fabulous Clip-n-Save Phone Call Response Chart

HIM	YOU
"I was such a horrible boyfriend. I treated you like crap. I didn't deserve you."	(*Click.*)
"I'm not that person anymore. I'm a new man."	(*Click.*)
"Since we split up, my life has been hell. I lost my job, my dog died . . ."	(*Click.*)
"I have to see you. If I don't see you, I might do something drastic."	(*Click.*)
"Hi, it's . . ."	(*Click.*)

12

The Dangers of Destiny

"He Called While I Was Thinking About Him. Therefore, We Are Meet to Be"

I THOUGHT IT might be prudent to say a few words about destiny. Believing in destiny has caused many a strong woman to go back to a guy who's a complete putz.

Yes, women see destiny in the darndest places. Here are some of the things women told me they took as "a sign that I was meant to get back together with my ex":

▲ Running into their ex at a mutual friend's wedding
▲ Running into their ex outside the apartment complex where they both live
▲ Running into their ex in the office where they both work
▲ Running into their ex as they jogged past his house for the 13,000th time
▲ Running into their ex as they broke into his apartment in a vain attempt to retrieve their contact lens case.

For one woman, geography was destiny. "After I moved to New York from Boston, I discovered that I'd moved across the street from my ex and that I could even see into his apartment if I used my extra-strength binoculars, leaned way out the window, and twisted my neck painfully."

Coincidence? Perhaps. Bad luck? Maybe. But *fate?* I think not.

Some women even think that *good sex* indicates destiny. "My ex had such a perfect penis," one woman told me. "No one's penis is as perfect as his. I think our bodies are meant to be together."

I tried to explain to this woman that there are lots of nice-looking penises out there, but she wouldn't, er, bite. Destiny had once again reared its ugly head.

Believe it or not, I, too, have turned to destiny for an answer to my relationship problems. Actually, I'm thinking of one breakup in particular. I had initiated the split and was feeling kind of conflicted, because while I realized that my ex and I didn't have much in common, I was still fairly attracted to him.

In other words, there was a part of me—a part that shall remain nameless, because my parents are reading this—that really regretted the breakup and wanted me to go back to my ex.

This conflict, which historians later dubbed The War of the Head and Hormones, went on for quite a while. Sometimes the head would, well, pull ahead, and I'd go for a few days without thinking about my ex at all. Then the hormones would launch a surprise attack and bombard my brain with messages like, "Call him! Have him come over! If you don't, we will make an extremely offensive strike to your nether regions!"

Unable to make a definitive decision, I turned to the fates for advice. I read every horoscope I could get my hands on, looking for clues as to whether or not I should call my ex. I had my tea leaves read. I started taking the fortunes in my fortune cookies seriously. I even went so far as to create my own version of that fortune-cookie game, the one in which you add the words "in bed" to the fortune to give it a whole different meaning. Only I added the words "in your relationship with your ex."

A fortune that read, "Sing a song. Your creative juices are flowing" now read, "Sing a song. Your creative juices are flowing *in your relationship with your ex.*"

"Happiness begins with a smile and a wink" became "Happiness begins with a smile and a wink *in your relationship with your ex.*"

And "Romance will come in a very unusual way" meant that "Romance will come in a very unusual way *in your relationship with your ex.*"

Clearly, I needed professional help. So I did what any borderline sane woman would have done in this situation: I went to a fortuneteller and got my palm read.

"You will be meeting a strange man," she told me, staring at the lines on my palm.

I looked into my palm, too, but I couldn't see a damn thing. "What does this man look like?" I asked.

"He is dark and kind of tall," she replied. "I see a wedding happening. *(Pause.)* That will be $15."

"The wedding?"

"No, my bill."

I paid her and went home, my brain working furiously. "She was definitely talking about my ex!" I thought to myself. "He has *dark blonde* hair, and 5 feet, 6 inches is kind of tall! We must be destined to be together!"

Thankfully, reality set in. "Dark," I realized, could mean anything from dark-haired to tan to just plain moody. "Kind of tall" could mean anything from 5 feet, 4 inches to 7 feet. And "strange man" could mean anyone from the pizza delivery guy to an inmate at a mental institution.

I sadly faced the fact that my "fortune" was so vague that the fortuneteller could have been making the whole thing up. And even if she wasn't, it was possible that I had misconstrued the message entirely.

An episode of *Tales from the Crypt* illustrates this point.

Scene 1: Demi Moore goes to a fortuneteller, who tells her that she will marry a big man who's going to inherit $1 million.

Scene 2: Demi goes to work and meets a grotesquely fat guy who has really big lips. Assuming that this is the millionaire-to-be, she flirts with him. He falls in love with her, being as she's the only woman in a thousand-mile radius who'll give him the time of day (also, she looks pretty good).

Scene 3: The fat guy proposes and Demi accepts, although she refuses to have sex with him because he looks like a beached whale, only fatter.

Scene 4: Soon after the wedding, Demi goes grocery shopping and wins $1 million. (Hey, it's TV.)

Scene 5: Demi runs home, thinking that she'll finally be able to get away from her awful husband. Husband catches her packing and begs her not to leave. She won't listen. He chokes her. She dies.

Scene 6: Husband inherits her million, thereby becoming a millionaire.

Okay, so this is an extreme and incredibly unrealistic example. I still believe we need to rethink the whole fortunetelling thing. I mean, let's be honest: The only reason we women seek out fortunetellers is so we can find out if we're ever going to get married. And after a breakup, hearing that we're going to marry our ex is better than hearing *nothing about marriage whatsoever.* Fortunetellers know this. They learn it at fortuneteller orientation. "Here are the only four things you'll ever need to know about fortunetelling," say their teachers. "Number one: Always tell women they are about to meet a stranger. Number two: Always tell them this stranger will be tall and dark. Number three: Always tell them you see a wedding happening soon. And number four: Always, always wear gold hoop earrings. Class dismissed."

Some would argue that fortunetellers are doing us a favor, because they give us hope for the future. That may be true. But after a breakup, when you're feeling really vulnerable, they can also make you hope for the *wrong* future. Besides, believing in fate is a cop-out: It makes you think you don't have to take responsibility for your life.

For all of these reasons, I think that believing in destiny should come with the following warning label:

> **Warning:**
> Do not attempt to believe in destiny while you are suffering from a breakup. If you believe in destiny, do not drink alcoholic beverages or operate heavy machinery. And under no circumstances should you call your ex while you are believing in destiny, especially if you are operating heavy machinery and drinking at the same time. This can be very dangerous.

In summary, believing in destiny can make it harder to get over an ex. So, for the time being, try to avoid horoscopes, tarot cards, numerology, fortunetellers, and having anyone "read" the bumps on your head. Remember: If you and your ex broke up, then something was really wrong with your relationship. Therefore, it may be your destiny to *meet someone else*.

13

Movies, Books, and Songs You Should Seek Out During This Phase

(And Those You Should Avoid Like the Plague)

▲▲▲▲▲▲▲▲▲▲▲▲▲▲▲▲▲▲▲▲▲▲▲▲

Movies to Watch

▲ Trashing His Stuff movies—*Earth Girls Are Easy* is a good example: After her ex cheats on her, Geena Davis burns his record albums and rolls a bowling ball into his computer screen. It's cathartic just watching.

▲ Movies about women achieving independence, such as *Desperately Seeking Susan*, *Ruthless People*, and *Thelma and Louise*.

▲ He Came Back and She Didn't Want Him movies, such as *The Heiress* (starring Olivia de Havilland and Montgomery Clift). The *Halloween*, *Friday the 13th*, and *Night-*

mare on Elm Street series will also mentally prepare you for your ex's return.

▲▲▲▲▲▲▲▲▲▲▲▲▲▲▲▲▲▲▲▲▲▲▲

Movies to Avoid

▲ Made for Each Other movies, including *Sleepless in Seattle*, *Heaven Can Wait*, *The Butcher's Wife*, or anything involving destiny or fate.
▲ Any movie in which the characters break up and get back together (*About Last Night*, etc.).
▲ Movies that make you feel desperate or resentful, including *Splash* (even a frigging mermaid can get a man—what's *my* problem?) and *An Officer and a Gentleman* (woman finds love while spinster friend sobs).

▲▲▲▲▲▲▲▲▲▲▲▲▲▲▲▲▲▲▲▲▲▲

Books to Avoid

▲ Romance novels: At this stage, they might make you think, "Hmm. Maybe my ex *was* like Fabio, only I didn't notice it!" (This is known as the Diamond-in-the-Rough, So-Rough-It's-a-Cubic-Zirconia syndrome.)

▲▲▲▲▲▲▲▲▲▲▲▲▲▲▲▲▲▲▲▲▲▲▲▲

Songs to Listen To

▲ Get Lost—I Can Live Without You songs: Among them: "Enough Is Enough," "You Keep Me Hanging On," and the ubiquitous disco anthem "I Will Survive."

▲▲▲▲▲▲▲▲▲▲▲▲▲▲▲▲▲▲▲▲▲▲▲

Songs to Avoid

▲ Getting Back Together songs: "We Can Work It Out," "Why Can't We Be Friends?," and "Reunited," by Peaches and Herb, of course.

Part Three

Nine Months to One Year Later:

Okay, You're Really
Starting to Get Pathetic

6 Signs That You Should Run, Not Walk, to the Nearest Therapist*

▲ You continue to refer to men as "Those odd people with the strange-looking hangy-down things."

▲ Every song on the radio still reminds you of your ex, to the point that you've developed carpal tunnel syndrome from changing stations.

▲ You watched an episode of Oprah with the theme "Eighty-nine-year-olds who are still stuck on their high school sweethearts" and thought, "That will be me."

▲ Conversations with your new boyfriend go something like this:

YOU: That's funny. Derek used to say that, too.

NEW BOYFRIEND: Derek, Derek, Derek! Everything is always Derek! Derek this and Derek that! Well, I'm not Derek! And what's more, I don't *want* to be Derek! In fact, I *hate* Derek! I wish Derek would die! No—I wish he had never been born! The world would be a much better place without Derek! *(New boyfriend then falls to his knees and raises his arms toward heaven.)* Why, God? Why did there have to be a Derek? *Why?*

▲ You don't *have* a new boyfriend because, ever since the breakup, you *still* haven't come out of your bedroom.

▲ You spend your Saturday nights sitting in your rocking chair with a gray wig on your head, holding a butcher knife and mumbling, "He'll come back. I know he will."

*Or at least keep reading this book.

14

What to Do If It's Been a Really Long Time and You *Still* Aren't Over Him

"I HAVE STRONG feelings for six men from my past: My very first boyfriend, the guy after that, the guy after that, my son's father, my husband, and another boyfriend," said one woman. "I think about each of these guys at least once a month."

Okay, so I admit that this woman's case is a little extreme. The fact remains that there are many women out there who still aren't over guys they dated months and months ago. If you're one of them, this chapter's for you.

▲▲▲▲▲▲▲▲▲▲▲▲▲▲▲▲▲▲▲▲▲▲▲▲▲

Four Possible Reasons Why You Can't Forget Him

1. **Your relationship never technically ended.** One of the really annoying things about men, at least in my experience, is that

they tend to avoid saying goodbye. They don't like finality. My theory is that they like to keep their options open. "I don't want her right now, but in a few years or so, maybe I *will*," they think.

This is all well and good—for *them*. Unfortunately, it keeps *us* from getting the closure we need. "When my boyfriend and I split up, there was no discussion, no fight, no nothing," one woman told me. "The circumstances were such that I was always wondering if it would have worked out. If we had had some sort of closure, it would have taken me a more reasonable amount of time to get over him. Instead, it took more than three years, even though I dated other guys like crazy."

"My high school sweetheart and I lost touch when he and his family moved away," said another woman. "I've been trying to find him for the last twelve years. I even hired a private investigator! I just want to see how he turned out and wish him well."

"I never got a straight answer from my ex about *why* he dumped me—he just kept saying it was 'bad timing,'" said another. "Ever since, I've thought, 'If I'd just met him six months sooner, or six months later, we'd probably be married now.'"

Worst-case scenario: Your ex abandons you completely, without a word. So many women I talked to had had this happen to them that I began to suspect that their exes were all the same guy—Boyfriend X, if you will.

"I dated my ex for a year and a half," said one woman. "Then one day, he just disappeared. I left messages at his home and his office, but he never returned my calls. He wouldn't answer the door at his apartment, either. Three years went by, and in that time period I couldn't sleep and my whole balance was off. Then one day I ran into him on the street, and it was like I'd seen Jesus. Of course, he acted like nothing had happened and that he'd just talked to me the day before."

"My husband deserted me—he just walked out one day," said another woman. "I couldn't get in touch with him, because I didn't know where he was. It took me seven months to file for a divorce, because I kept waiting for him to come back."

Said another: "My ex just woke up one morning and said 'I can't do it.' I thought he meant he couldn't make coffee. Turns out he was talking about the relationship—he just went out the door and kept on walking."

Where do boyfriends go when they disappear? Nobody really knows for sure. Maybe they're floating around in some black hole with your missing socks. Then again, maybe they're simply hiding out in their apartments like the rats they are.

2. You have lingering regrets. Sometimes you can't let go of a relationship because you did something you're ashamed of. One woman couldn't forgive herself for changing her *name* to please her ex. "I've always gone by Maggie, but I started going by Margaret because my ex told me he liked it better," she said. "I completely embarrassed myself in front of my friends. They kept hanging up on my machine because they thought they had the wrong number: 'Margaret? Who the hell is Margaret?' I totally lost my own identity."

"I can't forgive myself for being such a doormat," said another woman. "My live-in boyfriend would go out at night and come back in the morning wearing different clothes, and I wouldn't say a word. The thought that he's still laughing at me keeps me up nights."

And another woman told me: "I'm the one who cheated; my boyfriend found out and that was the end of it. I felt like such a bad person. Still do. I never got to apologize."

3. You miss the lifestyle. Sometimes it's not really your ex that you miss—it's the you you used to be. "Our relationship was so idyllic," said one woman. "For two years, we lived in a house on the beach. It was a golden time. We were totally out of control and just lived for the moment. We felt so *free*. Now my life is just the opposite—and I've become obsessed with thoughts of my ex."

4. Your ex is still a part of your present. It's pretty hard to get over a guy when you're still paying the price of dating him—literally. One woman's ex took $2,500 out of her savings account when he left; she bounced so many checks that her credit rating was ruined. Another woman bought a brand-new truck; her ex drove off in it and never came back. "I later found out he sold it for $700," she said. "It still burns me up—I'll be paying it off for the next ten years."

It's also hard to get over someone when you have his child, work with him, or still live together.

Yes, I said live together—and it's more common than you'd think. One woman told me that she and her live-in shared an apartment for three whole months after the split. "It was utter hell," she said. "We didn't even speak to each other. I never wanted to go home."

Another woman lived with her husband for two months

after he told her he wanted a divorce. "I wanted him to change his mind," she said. "I'd make him breakfast and kiss him goodbye as if nothing had changed. It was so stressful."

And one woman's husband stayed on even after the divorce was final. "He won't even talk about leaving," she said. "He just acts like nothing has happened—and I'm too chicken to bring it up again." For all we know, he's *still* there.

I think we can all agree that the above situations are about as healthy as ordering *fugu* at a fast-food restaurant. If you're still not over the guy (or the relationship), it's time for drastic action. Remember the Law of the Vacuum: "Electric shock could occur if used outdoors or on wet surfaces."

Oops! Wrong law! What I meant to say was, "To make room for something new, you have to clear a space."

As one woman explained it, "Unfinished business drains your energy and keeps you from moving forward with your life. If you don't take steps to end it, you'll kill all the good memories."

Truer words have not been spoken. Well, okay, they have—just not in this book. At any rate, if your previous attempts at making a clean break failed miserably, you might want to use one of the following tried and true techniques.

> *Warning:* Some of these tactics are rather severe. Attempt them at your own risk. In other words, if they don't work, don't come crying to me.

TACTIC #1: Speak your piece. If your ex left you without an explanation or the relationship ended in anger, chances are you can't get closure because you never got to express your feelings fully. If this is the case, tell your ex how you feel. If the thought of doing this face-to-face makes you squeamish, try mailing your ex a registered letter. "I was afraid I'd weaken if I saw my ex in person," said one woman. "So I analyzed him and our relationship on paper and sent it registered mail. Just seeing the return receipt with his signature was closure enough."

You can also try using a third party. "I apologized to my ex through his sister," said another woman. "I told her, 'I was young, I was immature, I feel bad for how I acted. Tell him I'm sorry and that I wish him the best.'"

TACTIC #2: Pretend he's dead. Lay your ex to rest, if not literally, then at least figuratively. Here's how one woman did it: "I threw a fake funeral for my ex a year after the breakup. I bought a sexy black dress and invited all my friends to the 'wake.' First we shared funny stories about what a blithering idiot my ex was. Then we used his picture to play Pin the Tail on the Ex. Later, we tore up the picture, put the pieces in an envelope, and ceremoniously buried it in my back yard. It was quite a joyful occasion."

TACTIC #3: Cut yourself off from his friends and family, too. I thought this went without saying, but one woman told me her ex's sister cuts her hair, and another said she was *still* sending Christmas cards to her ex's parents. "Why stop there? Why not just crash his next family reunion?" I wanted to ask.

TACTIC #4: Get a divorce. "My ex and I lived together for five years," said one woman. "After we parted, my friend

Marge drew up some phony divorce papers and had me sign them. It made the ending seem much more final."

TACTIC #5: The closed-door policy. "My husband and I have joint custody of our kids," said one woman. "He used this as an excuse to call me constantly, which made me

> "One thing that made the breakup especially hard is that I really loved his parents and they loved me. They wanted us to get married. It was hard to let them go."
> —Dalena, Los Angeles

feel very conflicted. I didn't think there was any way to finish it—until a friend told me about her closed-door technique. First, you envision your ex and everything you feel about him; then you picture a solid closed door. This really works. After a while, you will begin to feel at peace with yourself and the relationship—and believe me, your ex will sense the vibes."

TACTIC #6: Move to another city. If your ex is harassing you, or if every single building and sidewalk square in your town sparks a memory of him, it's time for the Permanent Escape. Here's how to do it: ▲Spread rumors that your company gave you a huge promotion and is transferring you to L.A., and that they'll be paying the rent at the fabulous Melrose Place–like apartment complex you'll be moving into. ▲Buy one of those life-sized male dolls from the Safety Zone catalog,* put it in the front seat of the U-Haul, park in front of

*Call 800-999-3030 to order.

your ex's house on your way out of town, and mash with the doll until you're sure your ex has seen you.

"I moved to Florida to get away from my ex," said one woman. "It was wonderful! It gave me an entire change of scene—and knowing that I wasn't ever going to run into him was a *huge* relief."

The most important thing about these tactics is that they put *you* in control. And once you realize you're in control, you will no longer blame your ex for ruining your life. This will keep you from becoming a bitter person.

A lot of people think they have to hate their ex in order to get closure—but actually the opposite is true: Hating someone keeps them with you longer. Besides, hate makes you feel like crap. It's what causes murder, war, and the best episodes of Oprah.

Indifference is what we're after. We're going for that place where you can run into your ex on the street as he's proposing to his new girlfriend, Christy Turlington, and instead of wanting to scratch both their eyes out, you'll think, "Better her than me."

People say happiness is the best revenge. Not me. Who wants to see their ex with Christy and think, "I'm so happy for him"? Nope, give me indifference any day. He doesn't deserve your blessing, the scum.

Note: If you're having a problem with the hatred thing, it may help you to remember that no relationship is *all* bad. Each one teaches you something or brings some enjoyment into your life. At the very *least*, it will give you something to draw on in the event that you become a famous actress.

15

Getting Involved Again

Emotional Baggage—Are You Over Your Weight Limit?

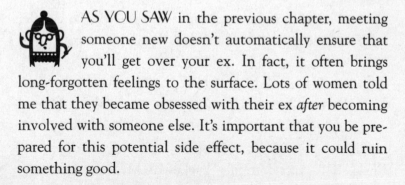

It's your first trip with your new boyfriend, and you're carrying two suitcases.

HIM: Honey, you brought way too much luggage.

YOU: Oh, that big one's just my Emotional Baggage.

AS YOU SAW in the previous chapter, meeting someone new doesn't automatically ensure that you'll get over your ex. In fact, it often brings long-forgotten feelings to the surface. Lots of women told me that they became obsessed with their ex *after* becoming involved with someone else. It's important that you be prepared for this potential side effect, because it could ruin something good.

COMMON PROBLEM #1: Seeing your ex in the way he eats, dances, breathes. We tend to be attracted to certain qualities in people, so your new guy may have some of the same quirks as your ex. Maybe they both like to be the center of attention, or enjoy long-distance spitting, or refer to their sexual organ as their "trouser trout." (Hey, I never said these quirks had to be *pleasant.*) Some women are even drawn to men with the same *name:* One woman I know dated five Steves in a row.* This actually came in handy when she slipped up a few times in the heat of passion.

COMMON PROBLEM #2: Comparing the two and having your new guy come up short. There may be times when you wish your new guy was actually more like your ex. "My ex was a very good teacher," said one woman. "He taught me how to water-ski, how to play Frisbee. My husband, on the other hand, is very competitive; he'd never be able to say, 'You're doing great!'"

"My husband isn't as literary as my ex," said another. "Sometimes I have to explain things to him that my ex would have automatically understood. It's kind of disappointing."

And another woman told me, "My ex liked to cuddle, and I really miss that. My husband's not as affectionate."

COMMON PROBLEM #3: Letting your ex influence your behavior. "I don't really like to cook, and my ex always criticized me for it," said one woman. "In my next relationship, I felt like I had to get back at him, so I became a virtual Julia Child. This tactic totally backfired: My new boyfriend

*That is to say, consecutively.

thought I loved to cook and began to take my gourmet meals for granted."

"I really love ethnic food, so I was thrilled when my new boyfriend took me to three exotic restaurants in one week," said another. "Later I found out that he hated ethnic food and had only taken me to these places to prove a point to *his* ex. I felt duped."

COMMON PROBLEM #4: Discovering you have an emotional allergy. I read in *Scientific American* that if a person's in a car accident in which the horn gets stuck in the On position, he or she may later have a reaction to the blaring of horns and become anxious or depressed as the emotional memory is activated. The same thing may happen if your new boyfriend does something that makes you recall a past trauma involving your ex. "Whenever my ex was lying, he used words that weren't normally part of his vocabulary," said one woman. "Even now, if my fiancé uses a word like 'hubris,' I get all tense."

Scientists have found that our emotions about traumatic events are stored in the same part of the memory that sets off the fight-or-flight response. This is because, in prehistoric times, recognizing threatening situations was crucial for physical survival. This still holds true, although nowadays it has more to do with *emotional* survival. Translation: If you recognize a potential problem early, you may be able to protect yourself from being hurt.

The only problem with this is that each time your fight-or-flight response is activated by something your new boyfriend inadvertently does, the same stress hormones are released, running down the same neural paths and binding you ever tighter to those bad memories. Eventually these stressful reactions will become part of your emotional makeup, and you'll need an Emotional Makeup Remover. The experts suggest taking a beta blocker called propanolol, which impairs emotional memory without impairing normal memory. I suggest a lobotomy.

If that's not possible, try using flash cards. Write the offending phrase or action on one side of an index card, and write or draw something neutral on the other side. Example: side one, "hubris"; side two, "Switzerland." Practice with the cards until all negative connotations fade.

COMMON PROBLEM #5: Making your current beau pay for what your ex did to you. When you wound someone like your ex wounded you, it's called "mirroring the injury." This is very spiteful. Also, it may cause a chain reaction: You do it to your new guy, he does it to his next girlfriend, and so on, until eventually *I* date the guy at the end of the chain and he does it to *me*. Whereupon I will track you down and slap you silly.

At least one of these problems is bound to occur when you date someone new. If so, try to keep it to yourself. If your new boyfriend finds out, it may become a sore spot in your relationship. With any luck, the lingering memories of your ex will pass. If your new guy asks you about your ex before then, you may want to follow the advice of Heather Locklear: "Lie, lie until you die."

16

Movies, Books, and Songs You Should Seek Out During This Phase

(And Those You Should Avoid Like the Plague)

▲▲▲▲▲▲▲▲▲▲▲▲▲▲▲▲▲▲▲▲▲▲▲▲▲▲

Movies to Watch

▲ Healthy Relationship movies (at this stage, they give you hope and keep you from thinking all men are evil). Good examples are *Murphy's Romance*, *When Harry Met Sally*, *The Goodbye Girl*, *The Accidental Tourist*, or any movie in which someone gets dumped, gets over it, and meets someone way better.

▲ Movies that underscore the importance of closure, especially *The War of the Roses* (marriage collapses into a vicious divorce battle over material possessions; neither spouse will move out of the house).

▲▲▲▲▲▲▲▲▲▲▲▲▲▲▲▲▲▲▲▲▲▲

Movies to Avoid

▲ Unrealistic romances: *Pretty Woman, Frankie and Johnny, Casablanca, An Affair to Remember, Jane Eyre, Arthur.* And avoid all Disney movies: There ain't no such thing as Prince Charming, babe.

▲▲▲▲▲▲▲▲▲▲▲▲▲▲▲▲▲▲▲▲▲▲

Books to Avoid

▲ Romance novels: At this stage, they may get you thinking that Prince Charming *does* exist. Thinking this is utter folly. Remember: Men are a highly imperfect species and don't even come with a money-back guarantee. (The minute you start thinking a guy is perfect, he'll do something incredibly disgusting, such as wearing a chartreuse shirt with maroon pants.)

▲▲▲▲▲▲▲▲▲▲▲▲▲▲▲▲▲▲▲▲▲▲

Songs to Listen To

▲ One woman recommended Peter Gabriel's *Us* album: "It's about his own marriage breaking up and his problems with relationships since," she said.

Another told me: "There's a Billy Joel song that

goes, 'In every heart there is a room / A sanctuary safe and strong / To heal the wounds from lovers past / Until a new one comes along.'"

I couldn't have said it better myself.

Afterword

You've just read pages and pages of true testimony from women across the country. The stories in this book were chosen for their cathartic qualities; I hope they either helped you realize that (a) you aren't alone, or (b) you don't have it as bad as you thought. Both concepts will set you on the road to healing.

I know that the vast majority of ex-boyfriend stories contained herein were fairly negative, and that by this point you may be wishing that all men would just beam back up to the mother ship and leave you alone.

Stop right there! It's time to reiterate the important point I made in the very beginning: MEN ARE FABULOUS. IT'S EX-BOYFRIENDS WHO STINK. Remember: Your exes are your exes because they were wrong for you, *even if they initiated the breakup*. (If they were right for you, they'd still be with you, right? Right.)

For the record, I'd like to tell you that most of the

women I interviewed have found men who are way better than their exes. Many are now happily married and can't believe they ever had to put up with their ex-boyfriend's crap. Others are dating guys who treat them with respect and care. And still others are choosing to be single for a while; they're holding out for a good man and have decided not to settle for anything less.

I fall into this last category, partly by choice and partly because as soon as I tell prospective dates I'm writing a book about ex-boyfriends, they run screaming down the street. (Feel free to use this technique the next time you want to get rid of some smarmy guy who's hitting on you.)

But I'm not bitter. In fact, I'm thrilled: After writing this book, I'm virtually baggage-free, and feel confident that exorcising my demons has put me on the road toward a better relationship. I hope my book has done the same for you.

If the concept of a baggage-free relationship seems just too weird, relax: Chances are, your next boyfriend will have *plenty* of baggage for you to deal with. Unless, of course, he's read this book.

Acknowledgments

I have so many people to thank that this is going to read like an Oscar Acceptance Speech from Hell.

Tough noogies.

I would first like to thank Betsy Radin, my fabulous editor, for plucking me out of virtual oblivion and saying, "I want you to write a book about ex-boyfriends." Betsy, you're the only person I've never had to prove myself to as a writer, and I'll always be grateful for that. Thanks!

I would also like to thank my dad, Tom, for his continued enthusiasm and encouragement. Thanks, Dad, for being with me all the way, and for supporting me not only in the writing of this book but in every other facet of my life as well. You are one of my best friends—and I'm very lucky to be able to say that!

Thanks to my mom, Jeannie, for spending hours on the phone with me during the writing of this book. Mom, you were a great sounding board. I really appreciate how you listened patiently as I read (and reread) every single word to you. Thanks for laughing in all the right places—that was the greatest encouragement of all!

Thanks to my adorable sister, Tammy, for taking the time to go through her "memory boxes" and tell me about her exes. Tammy, you have always been my hero, and now, as a nurse, you are literally a hero to others. I love and admire you so much!

Thanks to my fabulous friend Leslie Nilsson for telling me her own dating stories and for giving me an honest and helpful critique of the first seven chapters.

Special thanks to all of my friends and family who showed their support by letting me interview them: Leila Bowie, Dalena Ganakes, Jan Hennenfent, Julie Hillgartner, Amy Johnson, Beth Johnson, Pam Kohll, Jenny Kuster, Amy Mertens, Deb Nadolsky, Kris Roberson, Jaye Taylor, and Sue Vinella.

And thanks to the other women who shared their stories with me: Kyra, Jennifer, Maya, Shari, Petra, Dorian, Ilene, Wanda, Brenda, Kim F., Jackie, Linda, Juliet, Kim W., Angela, Carol, Shawna, Jeannie, Karen, Patty, Anne, Susie, Margaret, Dawn, Toni, Debbie, Lis, Elizabeth, Sabrina, Erica, Erin, and Susan. I had so much fun talking to you!

Thanks to everyone in the ever-expanding Kuster and Brown clans for all the love, support, and affection you've given me over the years. I love you all!

Special thanks to my great-grandma, Georgia Baker, and my wonderful grandparents: Jeanette Kuster and Bernice and Claude Brown.

Thanks to my loving Brooklyn family, the Scottos, for taking care of me over the years.

Special thanks to Stephen Scotto, math genius, for helping me come up with a Post-Breakup Equation that really works.

Thanks to my friend Sunil Verma for lending me his computer when mine broke, for helping me format the original proposal, and for giving me emotional boosts when I was suffering from writer's block.

Thanks to my agent, Laura Blake, for taking me on—no questions asked—and helping me with all the legal mumbo-jumbo.

Thanks to Sarah Gilbert for directing me to Laura, helping me with the proposal, and bolstering my confidence.

Thanks to Andrew Postman for the sage advice and encouragement.

Thanks to my fabulous friends Kathi Cook, David Dobzelecki, Lisa Galvin, and Angela Glasgow for giving me names of women to interview.

Thanks to everyone at *Glamour* magazine—especially Judy Daniels—for giving me my start as a magazine writer.

Special thanks to Christine Fellingham for being so supportive.

Thanks to Pam and Jeff Brick for their enthusiasm.

Thanks to my new friend SARK for her intuition and inspiration.

Thanks to the town of West Burlington, Iowa, for being such a wonderful, safe place to grow up.

And, last but not least, thanks to all of my ex-boyfriends for being so wrong for me. If any of you had worked out, this book would not exist and I would not be the fabulous success I am today.